Photographing Dogs
Sally Anne Thompson

First published in Great Britain August 1989 by
Hove Foto Books
34 Church Road
Hove, Sussex BN3 2GJ

German Edition by Kynos Verlag, Eifel, August 1989

British Library Cataloguing in Publication Data
Thompson, Sally Anne
   Photographing Dogs
   1. Photography. Special subjects: pets. Dogs.
   I. Title
   778.9'496367

ISBN 0-906447-49-6

Pagesetting by Icon Publications Limited, Kelso, Roxburghshire, Scotland
Printed by Schwabenverlag AG, Ostfildern, West Germany

Frontispiece – *Beagle standing with a cloudscape. This is the famous All-Time-Top-Winning Beagle, Ch. Too Darn Hot For Tragband, known as Ada. I took this picture at about nine o'clock in the morning and was fortunate in finding such a good cloud formation to frame the dog. Andrew Brace, her owner, arrived en route for the big Hound Show, to have her photographed for the front cover of the Dog World Annual. We went up to nearby Painswick Beacon where she took up various poses that pleased her, and then she went off hunting in dense undergrowth where foxes had been seen, plainly telling us that photography was over – she is a great companion as well as a show dog, and is allowed off the lead. By ten o'clock the sky clouded over for the day so if we had not been short of time, which necessitated and early start, the pictures would have been far less interesting. Luck always plays a part in animal photography, but one must be ready to take advantage of it.*

Contents

Introduction

My lifetime's work has been the photography of animals – all kinds of animals, ranging from wildlife in Africa to pet gerbils in cages, but dogs have been my favourite subjects, as well as companions and friends through my life.

I am often shown sets of prints by friends who are genuinely disappointed by the standard of their photography but are quite unclear as to how to improve it. Many of these pictures show errors such as camera shake, under- or over-exposure, faulty focus, tiny animals in vast backgrounds, heads or feet cut off, bad camera angle, poor positioning of the animal, inattention to background detail. However, far from being hopeless, the intentions are usually good, and with a little knowledge of aspects of photography that apply especially to dogs, pictures that are worthy of pride rather than apology can easily be produced.

I am often asked 'How ever do you get your pictures?' This book is an attempt to answer this simple question in, as far as possible, a simple way.

Apart from the technicalities, a variety of skills is involved which offer great scope for any talents or aptitudes the would-be dog photographer may possess. Dog photography can be considered as a cross between portraiture, sports photography and photo-journalism.

Overleaf – *Three shots that came about through good luck*
Left – *Two Beagle puppies dancing. Preparation and concentration are needed for active puppy shots. Decide in advance that you intend action and set the shutter speed accordingly, try to be a step ahead of the dogs in your judgement of their actions and take the picture just as they go into their best position. Visualise the movements of these pups before and after this shot and you will appreciate how one can anticipate the right moment.*
Bottom Left – *Two Harlequin Great Danes dancing. These dogs were always incorrectly called Dalmatians when this picture was much used in the heyday of black and white. Once again it is chance that dogs will play like this, but the photographer must be ready to seize the opportunity.*
Right – *While photographing this Bichon at a show the Pyrenean Mountain Dog joined in.*

An eye for composition plus speedy reflexes are needed. Take for example the day you are photographing your dog swimming in the sea. Suddenly he leaps from the water, grabs your child's ice cream, eats it and then sits down with a guilty yet self-satisfied look on his face. Action, a story and a portrait all within seconds, each a potential shot worth a book on its own, but all coming under the heading of dog photography.

I like dog photography for the way in which anything can happen, always with the chance of unexpected, wonderful shots appearing, often quite different from anything you had anticipated. I think that an element of luck always keeps you on your toes – there can be no retakes of most animal pictures – and a lost picture is something to mourn, if only temporarily.

But life can be made easier by being prepared. You are embarking upon a type of photography which generally is not well catered for by the makers of popular cameras and equipment. If you can reduce the technical worries by understanding your camera and making its operation second nature, then the pictorial and creative side can have your full attention.

In this book I will discuss how to get better pictures and achieve a professional standard of work but with special emphasis on helping the complete beginner using a simple camera. I have chosen many of my favourite illustrations, and have include some of my failures which well illustrate how not to do it. These are all from actual jobs where I thought at the time I was doing well and had secured satisfactory shots.

I hope all this will help to bring you the pleasure of taking good photographs of dogs – your own, your friends' and possibly your clients'. It is a way of life that I have enjoyed for many years and can thoroughly recommend.

CHAPTER 1

My type of picture

I well remember the feeling of nervousness and excitement on the day my father loaded up a box camera for me and put it into my hands saying 'Hold the camera still and point it in the right direction'. I was still at school, aged about 12, and the first pictures I took were of dogs. Of course they were not great masterpieces and the dogs' owners did not see them. I have not given these pictures thought until now, but I can still remember how I was drawn to the subject.

Yorkshire Terrier

Our family business was fashion photography, so I grew up among photographers, but no one, including myself, thought of my dog and horse pictures as anything more than a hobby, and a rather inconsequential one at that. I was always very keen on photography and after leaving school I worked as general assistant in our studio, but it was very much against my father's wishes because he saw photography as an overcrowded profession and really wanted me to take up something else. The trouble was that I was not interested in fashion at all, but was unsure of what to do next.

No doubt we all need a stroke of luck and mine came when our studio was asked to supply some photographs of English dogs for the French publishers Larousse. This was most unusual as our fashion photographers knew very little about dogs, but we had connections with the French publishing houses through my father's partner, Scaioni, who had a studio in Paris, and we were sometimes asked to undertake

Below left – Paddy. This little dog was taken on my 4x4 Rolleiflex. He belonged to a teacher at school. His is my earliest published picture – it was used in a calendar. Below right – Irish Water Spaniel. Taken on my Agiflex at an outdoor dog show. In my early days I always liked this picture for its sharpness and detail in the hair – the coat of this breed lends itself well to a close-up. The clasp of the lead detracts slightly, but some shots are taken quickly without the opportunity to arrange such details. The use of this picture in an advertisement was the beginning of our photo library.

Irish Wolfhound and Whippet

Afghan Hound

Borzoi

Smooth Collie

Above – *Shows provide a great chance for dog photography. At larger events the dogs are benched and you can wander among them looking for a picture, as I did at Crufts many years ago. The dogs cannot be moved in any way because no one is allowed to touch them unless the owner is present, so you take natural pictures as they crop up. For the Borzoi and Collie I used my Rolleiflex and the other two were taken some years later during an assignment for* The Field *magazine. All were lit with a single flash on a bracket alongside the camera which is satisfactory especially where the shadow is lost on a dark background. In monochrome 'red eye' can be retouched – the only one showing any sign of it was the Irish Wolfhound.*

commissions. Miss Vera Watkins' 'Windswift' Salukis, in Kent, were picked as our models and I was allowed to go along as assistant on this job. Naturally I took my camera, a small format Rolleiflex, and after the official pictures, Miss Watkins asked me to take some of her dogs. This was my beginning. She is a remarkable woman, full of ideas, and has set several people on the road to a successful career. She told me about the world of dog showing and arranged for me to take a tent as a trade stand to display my work at a dog show. She encouraged me in many ways and commissions slowly came in, which I was able to undertake whilst working in the fashion studio.

Our picture library was born when I was asked for a photograph of a dark dog to be superimposed on a television screen for advertising in a catalogue. There were fewer picture libraries around in those days,

Left – Lioness in a tree after a good meal, Lake Manyara National Park, East Africa. This is one of the best sellers from our amateur safari.
Below – Caucasian Sheepdogs. While waiting for the Kabardine horses to be rounded up for my pictures in the Caucasus Mountains, near Piatigorsk, in the south of the USSR, I was thrilled to find this dog with a bullock cart preparing to depart. It was difficult to find out anything about the dog; he was just a worker, but his cropped ears are interesting.

the late 1950s, but I realised that this would be a good outlet for my pictures, I began to file everything carefully and keep my records in a small note book.   When I look at our large filing cabinets full of thousands of transparencies and our computerised records, it is amusing to think of those small beginnings.

A few general picture books of dogs were published at that time, but the majority were of show dogs in formal poses – all looking rather artificial. Beside these quite stuffy books was the opposite extreme, the so-called funny books with pictures of puppies falling in the water and other disasters. The popular style was of table-top photography – puppies in the straw, kittens in baskets, all on a table with studio lighting. I was far more keen on dogs in the open countryside. I liked to depict them in a way that showed their breed type and character, but at the same time looking natural in a pleasant pictorial shot. So these were the pictures I tried to take. I was having some success with my photography of show dogs for their owners, but no publisher was impressed and I had to accept people looking at my favourite shots and expressing great disappointment that the dogs were not 'sweet' enough. But eventually, luckily for me, tastes changed and my style of picture slowly came into demand.

By now I had progressed to an Agiflex, a single lens reflex, with 6 x 6cm format. I wonder how I ever managed a good colour picture because the lens had to be stopped down manually for each shot after focusing, and the camera was not sufficiently well balanced to be hand-held and so always had to be on a tripod. My father was a hard taskmaster. I was never indulged and had to work for everything but he must have had faith in my work because he bought me a Hasselblad. From then on I knew I had no excuses and was honour-bound to make a success of my photography.

Funnily enough it was a photographic safari to East Africa which really established my career. Safari is not really the correct description because it was amateurish in everything except the pictures we took. I went with my brother: we were complete innocents in Africa – we got stuck in the mud in our hired car with lions roaring around us, and we ran out of petrol in the highlands in an area where you were likely to be shot. But we did quite well and the pictures are still being published now, 20 years later. I think that photographing wild animals is good training: it teaches you to wait and watch. There is nothing you can do, or should do, to change anything the wild animal does, so you simply have to think ahead and read his mind. Recently I said to an owner after a session with a Bloodhound, 'It was like photographing a wild animal, which I really enjoy'. This needed explaining as she was taken aback at this description of her lovely hound, but the point was that the dog had cast about, as Bloodhounds do, oblivious to commands, doing exactly as he wished in the quarry where we were working. I did a lot of running and photographed him when I could, with a telephoto lens. The results were pictures that could not have been posed and were completely typical of this breed.

An important commission came after our return from East Africa when I was asked to illustrate a book Champion Dogs of the World. This in itself was not exceptional but the 'of the World' gave me the opportunity to see the top dogs of Europe and the USA, and photograph them off the lead – quite a feat! I was very grateful that the publishers of this book thought that its success merited another two in the series, first cats and then horses. To find the 'horses of the world' I had to range even further afield and I was able to make the acquaintance of Russian dogs when I had a moment to spare – among them the Moscow Guard dog, and the Black Terrier. I also saw the Russian sheepdog, the Owtcharka, in the mountains of the Caucasus.

Since those days I have met and admired dogs of all types. The show dogs have been glamorous and thrilling to photograph, but they are just dogs at heart and capable of giving as much love and companionship as the most affectionate pet. I think this fact has to shine through in pictures. It is my type of picture and I shy away from the slightest idea of making fun of the dog or demeaning him in any way.

Right – *Komondor on a farm. In my travels I always look out for dogs and met this Komondor on a farm in Hungary where I was photographing horses. It is difficult to find out about working dogs in some countries because so often they are seen as 'just the farm dog' and the owner becomes embarrassed and even suspicious if you show an interest and want to take photographs.*

choose the right camera or make a simple addition to you own equipment.

Backgrounds are almost as important as the dog himself, so I have given a great deal of thought to advising on the ones I have found best for the variety of tones and colours one finds with dogs. Dogs on the beach, in the woods or on a walk in the hills all make lovely shots, and on a beautiful summer's day what could be more pleasant than to try getting good photographs of them? I am glad I did not choose to become a news photographer who may have to spend a lifetime standing in city centres in the rain waiting for some dull public figure to appear!

There is one particular word that occurs very rarely in this book, and yet it describes the attribute so often ascribed to those who work with animals. Those possessed of it do not notice that they have it – without it my job would drive them mad. It is patience. But it need not be patience in everyday life; it is simply patience with animals. To take successful photographs of your dog you need endless patience, and to achieve this patience you must have a genuine affection for your subject.

But having implied that I am the most patient person with dogs I must admit that on some occasions I am spurred on by wishing to get the picture. I may see a wonderful shot through the viewfinder and for one reason or another fail to catch it. It could be my fault for being slow or perhaps the dog's handler is still in the picture, or the dog moves. Whatever the problem, I attempt to pose the dog again to recapture the picture I missed. All this makes one appear to have great patience, especially when the dog is really awkward, but it is the annoyance at losing a good shot that keeps one working and this suppresses any impatience.

CHAPTER 3

Posing the dog

There will be differences between the pictures that you take of your own dog and those of a professional taking show dogs. Many of the problems are similar, but I will write a little on the latter first.

No two dogs are the same – they vary in temperament, training and many other characteristics. They have their own ways and wishes, so their acceptance of your needs will likewise not be the same. A single cross word will demoralise some dogs while others can be admonished and shouted at but the smile will never leave their faces. I have to consider this with every dog I meet. It is really noticeable how considerate professional handlers can be to their dogs that require gentle treatment when they might feel they want to give the dog a smack.

As the photographer, and not the handler, I give my instructions but do not thrust my attentions or personality on the dog. This may seem surprising, because people who are successful with dogs are said to have a 'way with dogs', but my way with them is never to fuss or overwhelm. Be friendly, obviously, but once you start photographing you must incline towards pretending you are not there – if they love you too much they will run to you whenever you bend down to take the picture, which is infuriating. This, of course, is one of the worst problems when photographing your own dog and regrettably there is no real solution for it. Great tact is sometimes needed in my job to ensure that a happy atmosphere is maintained, as there is no doubt that dogs react to strained relationships between human beings. It is essential that no one gets angry and, when possible, husbands and wives should decide which of them is in charge of handling the dog.

Assume that a normal, stationary picture is being taken and that the dog will be standing in the place chosen for the picture. Most dogs look their best when alert and on their toes with ears and tail held correctly, according to their breed or type. Even the finest dog can look like a sack of potatoes if he is just hanging around, so his attention must be caught to get him to pull himself together and set his muscles rippling like a body builder taking up a pose.

Some dogs are no problem at all, but others may take a lot of waking

Above – *Miniature Wire-haired Dachshunds. Zena Andrews-Thorn poses her gang. It is not difficult to teach a dog to understand the word 'stay' – it is a necessity for a picture like this. The owner places the dogs and stays close to them. While she commands them to 'stay' the photographer attracts them with a suitable noise or action. I have aimed to keep the top of the dogs' heads just clear of the flower border, but in the heat of the moment a perfect background is not always achieved. The picture has to be taken very quickly once the handler draws back because most dogs are not fully trained in obedience, and not all will hold the pose for long. Within a group you will usually catch a few blinks or unattractive tongues, so a good picture is not easy.*

Right – *Smooth Collies. These dogs would have very much preferred a gallop to standing still, but eventually we achieved a picture. Should I give away that the dogs were on leads with the handler hiding in a hollow behind them?*

up. Noises are probably the most effective, from low growls to high squeaks but remember, and remind your helpers, that the noise must come from the direction in which you want the dog to look. You must not play all your cards at once or confuse the dog. Experiment to see what he likes; it may be a squeaky toy, a ball, a tit-bit or his dinner plate, a cat, a puppy, an enemy dog or a friend dog, door banging, car door opening, car horn, shouts of 'kill', 'seek', 'mark', or another dog's name. Or maybe he reacts to none of these. You can then go on to more sophisticated ploys, pretending to be the postman, milkman, dustman, maybe borrowing some geese or rabbits (all sorts of bad habits can be taught!). Keep trying – a tired Mastiff was once persuaded to look lively by a friend who lay on the ground and kicked his legs in the air. Some people did stare, but so did the Mastiff. You have to be prepared

This picture of a young Great Dane fails in many ways. Although the body of the dog shows up quite well the head is lost in the trees, particularly the ears. The shadow down the back of the neck and on the shoulder spoils the outline and dog should have been turned to avoid the shadow below the ribs. The lead looks very bad over the back although it vanishes nicely over the dog's hindquarters. Three points apply to the beauty of the dog herself – the feet are splayed due to the slope of the ground, the hindlegs are badly posed making her appear cow hocked, and her tail, which is normally correct has been caught at the wrong moment – a Great Dane's tail should not be carried high or curled.

to make a fool of yourself. My fellow professional photographers will agree that all this actually happens with show dogs to get the best out of them.

A pet dog, and this includes many show dogs since they too may be pets, will need only the slightest noise to gain his attention. Try different tones – a high pitched whining sound will often make the dog put his head on one side (an appealing pose but more suited to an appealing puppy than an adult of the nobler breeds). Then again some pet dogs have seen it all before and nothing will surprise them. If you are not having success, try moving to a different place. You may not have another background as good, but you should find some way to break the spell.

So much for alerting the dog, but he has to remain still and not run

Although still on a background which is not ideal for the head and ears, this picture is an improvement. The shadows on the dog's body have been eliminated giving her a cleaner outline, and it is interesting to see how much longer in back the dog now appears. The lead will be easy to paint out, but we have gained the handler's shadow. In colour I choose to disregard shadows on the ground and treat them as a necessary evil – in monochrome they are very easy to remove by retouching the negative. The position of the feet is vastly improved and although the tail is only just showing, it is correctly placed for this breed.

off towards the source of the attraction. Obedience-trained dogs, who might seem so perfect, in my experience may need special treatment, because while they are obeying their handler's orders they may not look happy or be able to relax. Dogs trained for work or show are usually easy to work with, but will only be good at their own thing. A show dog does not normally understand 'sit' because he is trained always to stand in the show ring, while a working gundog is encouraged to sit when holding a bird. Pet dogs with responsible owners should be well enough trained for the photographer to be able to snatch a picture,

Below – Ch. Aes Blue Dy-Almond For Movalian. An amazing name for an amazing little Chinese Crested bitch. Although the setting is unusual she revels in being the centre of attention and she posed beautifully with perfect expression and ear carriage. I am not a seeker of juxtopositions of textures but the coat-less dog and the rough stone do form an unusual combination.

Right – Norfolk Terriers

A typical group of Scotties from the famous Gaywyn kennels. Black dogs are often printed on a hard grade of paper giving greater contrast of tones to give detail in the black. If people are included in the picture the harsh printing is impossible since the faces would print too white: a softer grade of paper must be used, thus losing the brightness in the dogs. The background of this shot could be a little less cluttered but it is not too bad – one cannot remove flower beds from a garden with the wave of the hand, although careful retouching can accomplish it. The secret of six active dogs sitting so well together is revealed in the next shot – two tails each!

but others, especially if kennel dogs, may take advantage of the photography session as an opportunity for a good gallop as soon as they are let free. Sometimes when circumstance become really dire I attempt a bit of hypnotism/positive thinking: I announce to the dog 'YOU WILL STAY STILL AND NOT MOVE'. It works often enough to make it worth trying!

I think that a colour picture of a dog on a lead is less than pictorial, so it is worth going to great trouble to give the appearance of a dog standing free. If it is obvious that he is being held, and more so if he is strung up on a tight lead, the dog's character is diminished and the picture is poorer.

With black-and-white pictures the lead can be removed by retouching, but in colour this normally costs too much so some method of hiding it must be found. Very thin nylon or fishing line can be used but it must only be attempted with great care. For calm dogs whose owners have accustomed them to it, it works well, but for others one must be cautious. Even a small dog can become entangled in a thin line and for a big dog it can be dangerous, not only for the dog but also for the owner whose hand may be cut quite badly if the dog pulls hard.

It is important never to put a dog on a thin line when little puppies are around as they will get hurt if the dog thrashes about, and don't restrain a bigger dog on a long line when among people, as they can be knocked off their feet if the dog decides to move quickly. Be very careful what you tie a dog to. I remember a group of Pekingese and cats on a garden seat when at the last minute it was decided to add the pet donkey – tied to the seat. Something frightened the donkey and he took off, pulling the seat, scattering the cats and severely alarming the elderly Pekes. A nasty fright and never again. Do not persuade anyone to let a dog off the lead in an open place unless you are quite certain that it can be caught. I did this once with a very special Saluki in a London park; it was going to be a wonderful picture, but leaving my Hasselblad lying in the grass I ended up chasing the fleet-footed bitch as she disappeared towards the gates – and traffic. Again no harm was done but a lesson was learned. If a pony and trap or other vehicle is used in a picture with animals, it must be fixed so that the pony cannot move off; ideally a responsible person should be nearby in case of trouble.

For dogs that know not the word 'stay' I have a selection of leads about 3-5mm thick which I have dyed suitable colours for matching dogs and backgrounds. I fix the lead with a small tent peg to the ground behind the dog, and hope it will not show. Alternatively I tie the lead to a tree, bush or log and then draw the dog out in front of it, or sit him where the lead will be concealed. A background of long grass is ideal for hiding a lead and with a little imagination I am sure that anyone in their own garden or local park can find a good spot for photographs where the lead on a would-be runaway can be hidden.

Tails are very important; they indicate the mood of the dog but detract from the general outline of the dog if they are not right. Some breeds look well-balanced with the tail held straight out, level with their backs, which is their natural position when working. These are found among the gundogs: Setters, Pointers and Retrievers (except the Nova Scotia Duck Tolling Retriever who holds his tail above his back to attract the ducks in Nova Scotia!). Ways have to be found of contriving this correct tail carriage otherwise the dog will not be seen to its full advantage. We have even held up a Golden Retriever's tail by hand, uncomfortably, from within a wild rose bush. Calm and steady dogs can sometimes be placed in bracken or near bushes and their tails carefully propped up. Others can be persuaded to wag their tails and with careful timing and a fast shutter speed this can solve the problem. Have a conversation with the dog – 'good boy or girl' and so on, and the tail should wag. It is interesting that tail carriage is, to some extent, a matter of fashion. I watched the Gundogs at Madison Square Garden in New York where many of the Setters are encouraged to hold their tails high above their backs which is quite alien to experienced English eyes.

Some hounds, (Bloodhounds, Bassets, Beagles, for example), should

A large group with a horse and vehicle at Formakin Farm – a very carefully prepared picture with many animals, including a rabbit and a bird, aboard an Irish Jaunting Cart. For safety a chain has been attached to the axle of the vehicle and is fixed onto the tree on the right. This picture would only be attempted with a very steady horse and for added security the horse's handler was standing by the head out of shot.

An interlude during photography of a Rough Collie for a book jacket. The Collie would not concentrate in spite of everyone's efforts – we had made noises, shown him his dinner plate, and then the postman arrived. This is often a moment of value since most dogs relish the chance to have a grab at the letters – the postman co-operated and a spare camera was available for a quick shot of the proceedings.

hold their tails straight up because this is their pose when at attention on the hunt, but sensible dogs find no excitement in standing for a photograph and their tails will soon drop, so artificial methods must again be sought. I find it impossible with some dogs to achieve this tail carriage, so when it is not desperately important I give in and photograph the dog with his tail down. Dog-showing enthusiasts have become used to seeing all the tails in the correct mode because, in the past, photographs were in black-and-white and always had the hand holding the tail retouched out. This is normally too expensive in colour and has created a problem, but though I refuse to have a hand showing, I might allow the very tip of the tail, and the hand holding it, to be cut out of the picture. A branch can sometimes be used to nudge the tail up, as long as it looks natural.

It is an old custom in the trade to tie a thin line onto a tail to hold it in the correct position but I find that this is often unsuccessful. The line comes off the tail, the dog does not like it and humps his back and, if the focus is sharp throughout the dog, the line will show. It did work once though; the owner said that she always did it for pictures – and she knew what she was talking about as her dog was a Crufts Best in Show winner.

Some dogs are designed to hold their tails in a curl over the back; Norwegian Buhunds, Samoyeds and the other Spitz breeds, also Tibetan Spaniels, Tibetan Terriers, Pugs, Lhasa Apsos and Shih Tzus, Pomeranians, Pekingese, Japanese Chins, Keeshonds and Alaskan Malamutes. These Spitz breeds with their curled tails can be impossible to photograph when they drop their tails because it just illustrates an unhappy temperament and makes a bad picture, although the Siberian Husky's tail is carried down when at rest. The Puli always amuses me – his coat is corded and to stop his tail going down you just tie one of the cords on its back to a cord on the tail!

A great many breeds have to place their tails themselves, mostly because the tail is too short to manhandle. These would include the short-tailed terriers, the Schnauzers, the Boxer, and the docked tails of German Short-Haired and German Wire-Haired Pointers, the Weimaraner, and the Vizsla. The only way to photograph these dogs is to create the conditions for the dog to put his tail up – simple it may sound, but often impossible to achieve, and thereby stands the skill of the photographer. Breeds that have been docked in the past, but now have the full tail left on, will have a Breed Standard (the official description of the breed) to indicate the ideal look, but whether or not this can always be achieved in a photograph is doubtful.

However, it is not only photographic skills that are needed to bring success, but understanding and experience of dogs in these most specific circumstances. The vast majority of pictures are taken of dogs being their natural selves, and I sometimes suspect that professionals become slaves to traditions and customs that the amateur will not consider important in the least.

CHAPTER 4

Photographing your own dog

Photographing your own dog can in some respects be easier than photographing other peoples' dogs because you know him. But this is the very reason that makes it difficult to get a good picture. You are emotionally involved, your dog is one of the family, you do not have the detachment of an observer and you probably expect far too much from him.

I am able to write with feeling about photographing one's own dogs because it is something that I find very difficult to do myself. Unlike working with dogs owned by other people, I get very annoyed with my Norfolk Terriers when I cannot get them to co-operate, and I lose my patience with them and my family within minutes. I think the reason is that when working for someone else one has to put on a bit of a show! So this is my advice – work at it and while trying to create a feeling of calm, hope to persuade your dog to do as you wish. Better still ask a helper to do this while your finger is on the shutter release, but do not forget that you must first convince others of the importance of the picture and the need for common sense in what they do. So much depends on the handling of the dog. Some people can work wonders while others produce chaos.

The photograph which will be the most prized in the years to come is the one that really captures the essence of the animal, as you see him – but how elusive this special picture can be. One can love a certain look in a dog and feel that it is there for the taking, but when you produce

Overleaf Left – *I was grateful to the owner of this sweet Lakeland because, of the many people I had asked, she was the only one who would agree to bring her dog to pose for an undignified photograph of 'taking a dog's temperature'. This pet dog was specially bathed and trimmed for the picture and she looked so pretty that I took these extra shots for my library. The lighting is by one diffused flash in a large reflector near the camera, with a smaller direct flash high to the back on the left.*

Overleaf right – *I often walk with this Labrador, Katie, and her owner, and once in a while on a sunny day I take a camera. It was no trouble at all to sit her down with her best toy, a stick.*

the camera it is as though you had shouted 'dinner' or 'walk' – the spell is broken and the picture has gone. We seem to expect the dog to disregard our strange actions, like crouching on the ground at their eye-level, and we become annoyed at their curiosity and lack of co-operation in not keeping their distance. Prepared to be patient, we quietly creep up on him to shoot just as he gives a wistful gaze into the lens, but instead we find the dog licking our face with a wild-eyed expression – tempers are lost and the picture is further away than ever. So what price that great shot now?

When this happens it is easy to decide that any picture is better than none at all and settle for a couple of useless exposures, postponing

Left – Cross bred dog. Various aspects of a pet dog could be the caption. Actually this dog was a trained actor and had many parts in television and advertising. He was easy to photograph because his appeal is so obvious, he also sat still and his owners knew how to bring out his best expressions. These pictures are ordinary, every day shots you may say, but isn't that exactly what we try to take of our own dogs? If your dog jumps through fire and saves babies from drowning that's fine – but mine don't!

Below – Yes! Some dogs actually are trained to save babies! But both dog and baby will only do their act a couple of times for you so don't miss the shot! Naturally this was completely posed with the mother standing by, otherwise I would have been helping the dog and not behind the camera.

serious photography for another day. Now I would suggest that you do not give up but instead realise that this is a typical warm-up for professional and amateur alike. Your dog's behaviour would be only slightly different if photographed by me, and you at least have the advantage in knowing his ways. My advantage is that I expect to work hard for a picture and will not give up until I am sure I have achieved it.

One of the easiest pictures, and always a good one to take, is of your dog sitting in a favourite place; the picture should include the surroundings to remind you of the part the dog plays in the household. Of course in many of my photographs I am trying for a bit of an illusion. A Wolfhound appears to look nobly up to the hills while a Bulldog stands there, a figure of true grit, whereas a Maltese can be so beautiful that it hardly seems to be a real dog. If you let a squeaky toy or old feeding bowl come into the picture for this type of shot then the whole atmosphere is lost. But when you are taking a picture of your dog to record his everyday life it is very different. His old toys and favourite bowl are exactly what you would want to see in later years, so while I would clear away everything that looks too homely in my 'breed' pictures, for the pet dog at home I would leave the bits and pieces of memorabilia in the picture.

You may opt for a picture of your dog sleeping by the fireside or in your armchair, but he may well encourage you to improve his portrait

Left – *Dandie Dinmont with her ring. An example of photographing a dog doing her own thing.*
Below – *Dog shaking. Use the fastest possible shutter speed, a long focus lens so as to keep well away from the spray, and then anticipate your dog's actions.*

I am not fond of untrue stories made around a series of photographs but in this case I remember what happened. I first spotted the cat and dog lying on the seat together but decided to move the table in the foreground.

The two animals were on a torn rug and also on a background that I thought might merge with Sloopy. (I think now that this looks rather good but the tones were hard to judge at the time). Trusting that they would co-operate I put a length of white cloth over the seat but unfortunately neglected the lighting, resulting in harsh shadows which look far worse on this background than on the first one, left. In the picture on the right the shadow is better but it is totally the wrong moment, both animals are very bad and the blur of the cat's whiskers show that I was not using a flash of sufficiently short duration to stop all movement.

A reasonable shot at last! But there has been too much messing about, and the cat decides to leave.

by opening an eye with a quizzical look and challenge you to catch it before he falls asleep completely, or gets up and walks away never to take up quite such a good pose again.

What can I advise to improve the chance of success? Firstly I would tidy up my dog a bit. Give him a good brushing – perhaps he should have had a bath the day before – make sure his coat is gleaming and his whiskers and eyes are clean. Many dogs moult and shed their coats, so work out when yours will be looking really good and make a date in the diary to spend time on a picture. Coats that are normally stripped (rough coated terriers, for example) can look thicker and untidier in photographs than in real life making them appear scruffy and older than they are. So photograph these dogs just before they come into full coat. Heavily coated dogs like Rough Collies, Pyrenean Mountain Dogs and the Spitz breeds can seem to be in good coat, especially when it is just coming in, only for the camera to reveal that the coat is still sparse. So plan to take them only when you are certain they are in really full bloom.

When your dog is young and bright it is easy to imagine that he will never grow old. Well, maybe he will not in spirit, but get some pictures when he is in his prime. You will regret having nothing to remind you of those days once his face is grey and he has lost his springy step.

Photograph your dog doing his own thing – some dogs like a stick to carry, others may bring home the newspaper – a lovely shot. It may seem commonplace, especially if he does it every day, but this is all the more reason to have a record of it. We have a picture of our childhood dog sitting on his favourite step looking pleased, it couldn't be better as it brings back so many memories.

You may well have ideas of where your dog will enjoy himself, while being amenable to persuasion about standing still, and you may also have good equipment, but will it all add up to a picture that does justice to your dog? The answer may be no, unless you can see and react to that well-known and all important 'right moment'. The secret here is to imagine that you are playing a pin-table or computer game requiring split second timing and anticipation. You should visualise the picture and watch and wait like a hawk, aiming to release the shutter just as the dog comes into the right position, not waiting to confirm it.

Pictures are probably most often lost through delaying too long, so that the right moment is passed over and a good picture is replaced by a blurred figure as the dog makes his getaway. This right moment is so important, it comes and goes in a fraction of a second (which is all you need with a shutter speed of 1/250th or 1/125th). I think that in general there are far fewer 'right moments' with dogs than there are with people. Dogs have so many 'wrong moments' simply through being unable to understand what is wanted of them. No dog can be instructed to pull his most photogenic face for the camera, or to refrain from blinking or sticking his tongue out. Having said that, though, when I asked the owner of the wonderful Borzoi on the cover of this book why the dog was puffing his cheeks in and out, she said that she had told him to keep his mouth shut for the picture!

In deciding on the 'right moment' I always have to assess the standard of picture I am likely to get, in the same way that a portrait photographer of people does. If his sitter has great vivacity, charm and beauty the session may be one long 'good moment', although he should then be looking for the 'super right moment'. With a plainer subject the good picture takes much more searching out – a tutor on a course would tell you to look for the good features and accentuate them. That is fine with a human but with your dog there is not necessarily anything that you can pin-point as either good or bad. So if you have a dog, purebred or not, that is less flamboyant than some of the flashier breeds you may have to think quite carefully about how to bring out the best in him photographically. I will not give any examples but since 'beauty is in the eye of the beholder' I suggest that you concentrate on the aspect of your dog that attracted you to him in the first place, and try to capture this in your picture.

There are many dogs whose whole build and style will present you with the opportunity to take a picture without waiting for a particular expression. I am thinking of dogs like Basset Hounds whose wrinkles make them seem so sad, and others whose facial characteristics are thought to convey the temperament of the dog. We should beware of being too anthropomorphic and be selective when we interpret our dogs' expressions in terms of human feelings. A dog has his own character which we are trying to bring out. If we squeak a toy to make every dog put his head on one side with that quizzical, appealing look I believe we are selling him short. Puppies are an exception because all baby animals appeal to adults to protect and look after them, so I feel that a picture that shows this vulnerability and brings out our maternal instinct is all right, whereas in an adult dog it is somewhat patronising.

Keeping the dog still for a picture is always a problem but it is useful that dogs have the predisposition to remain stationary at times, as for example, do the pointing dogs. This is a version of hunting behaviour and so all breeds, including the terriers, will stop suddenly to look, listen, or sniff the air – all the more so if you are providing an interesting event to catch their attention.

Whenever you have the opportunity, take more than just one picture if the dog continues to be good. A dog poses perfectly for a picture so infrequently that when he does, instead of shouting 'got it', go on

The Salukis, as sight hounds, seem quite bemused by the activities of the terrier, an earth dog.

I had been commissioned to photograph these Salukis in the countryside and we decided that one of my Norfolk terriers might be good company for the Salukis for the pictures.

Top left – The hounds were fascinated by the terrier who showed no fear of them at all.

The two centre left pictures – The cream Saluki and the terrier became inseparable and played together all afternoon. Both pictures were taken at 500th sec. with plenty of panning. They were not taken with a motor but were single shots. The dogs then did a number of runs, being called on to gallop down the path in front of my camera.

Bottom left – My terrier now has a fir cone to amuse her, she was thrown it to encourage the dogs to run. The trees in the background may be thought obtrusive but I prefer not to be too fussy when the picture is otherwise good.

Top – Brakes full on for the Saluki as the terrier goes the other way necessitating the impossibility of panning in two directions at once!

Right – About four years later the two dogs met again and the caption must be 'don't you love me any more?', for, sad to say, my terrier rebuffed all the Saluki's advances and would not play.

Pekingese at her birthday party. Mandy, the Pekingese was an actress and was famous for her film parts. She had worked with, among others, Ingrid Bergman and Peter Sellars. But although she loved the show biz life and always played up to the camera, like all Pekes she had the heart of a lion – she was a devil for chasing ponies until her owners, John and Mary Holmes persuaded her that it was unsociable behaviour. For the last five years of her life she held a birthday party for her friends. This picture would have been easy with an automatic compact camera that balances daylight and flash. With less automation you should work out the correct aperture for your flash (in this case mainly to light the Pekingese who is unlit by the light from the window) then take a reading on the guests that are lit by natural light. Set the aperture calculated for the flash and the corresponding speed to expose the guests correctly. I used a small flash on the camera and admit to this being just a snapshot – but since it was a party and I was a guest it was not the occasion to introduce complicated lighting into the scene.

taking. See how it can be improved, by changing the angle, moving the camera position up and down and sideways and watch to see if the 'good' pose you photographed is actually a prelude to something better. I find that even if I manage to get a whole roll (twelve exposures) of the dog in the same stance, swiftly, and without pausing between pictures, it is surprising how different each shot will be. There will be blinks, an unattractive tongue when the dog has licked his lips or panted and the tail, the ears and the expression usually change between shots. Of course, where I have changed the angle, one viewpoint will turn out to be better, although I will not have had the chance to assess this fully at the time. In dog photography it is a terrible mistake to be mean with film. A feeling of freedom in the number of pictures you allow yourself to take, plus a willingness to waste some shots, is another secret of success. I am not advocating shooting many rolls of 35mm film of one subject with a motorised camera hoping that one of them will be good – that is stupid. I am suggesting that if the next picture is better than the last you should take it. If I am short of film (a rare happening because I usually take with me twice as much as I will ever need) I feel constrained and not able to take a chance with the shots. The need to conserve film means no picture must be wasted and this leads to hesitation and missed chances.

A walk with your dog can provide a good opportunity for pictures. Fill your pockets with everything photographic you will need, or sling a bag on your shoulder so that your hands are free. Take plenty of film

Salukis on the beach. Great scope for wonderful shots but not particularly easy because dogs will often pose at their best when out of reach of the camera, indeed they may hardly remain with you at all if they are as active as these two. Dogs that match the sand and sea in tone may not be as successful in dull light as these black and cream dogs.

together with fine leads, a comb, brush, towel, biscuits, ball, toys and possibly water for cleaning if your dog is of a pale colour and will look a mess if he gets muddy. Think carefully about whether or not to take along another dog for company. Now all you need is your running shoes and plenty of puff. Try to resist shouting the dog's name incessantly, or giving commands that he has not been taught. A dog should always be given some elementary training in 'stay'. It is extremely useful and could one day save his life. A dog who has been trained to 'stay' can be placed in any photogenic spot while you stand close by, willing and instructing him not to move, arranging some attraction to gain his attention. Ask a friend to help, or failing that, throw something for him to look at.

In Chapter 10 I mention the idea of the dog running from one person to another, and this can work well on a walk. In the same way, if your dog has been trained, or encouraged to jump, you could photograph him going over a log, a hedge or a stream – all of which can be very photogenic. Use a fast shutter speed and pan in the direction in which the dog is moving. Jumping towards you makes an effective picture, but focusing is more difficult. A zoom lens really comes into its own on a walk, since you are able to keep the dog a good size in the frame without your having to rush after him. But remember that a dog running around will often need different exposures to accommodate the changing lighting and background. In these circumstances an automatic exposure camera can be very useful and will enable you to get pictures that would otherwise be lost.

Water provides a chance for good shots but it can be difficult to pose dogs to advantage beside rivers. If your dog plays naturally in a river bed or climbs around on the stones this could be good, but an unwilling participant in 'messing about in a river' is a sad sight. A wet dog must look as though he is having a wonderful time otherwise he will just appear pathetic, although that can make a picture if your dog is prepared to be laughed at. Remember to protect the camera from the spray from your dog's shaking – but it makes an interesting shot using as high a shutter speed as possible to catch the drops of water flying off the coat.

Photographs taken on the beach are sometimes unsuccessful because the tones do not suit the colour, nor the temperament, of every dog. I am not thinking of exotic beaches or cliff scenes but just an ordinary shore with sand and sea. I find it most regrettable that so many beaches ban dogs during the summer. To me beaches and dogs were made for each other and I am sure that the majority of beach-goers welcome dogs, but it goes without saying that in all aspects of dog ownership we should ensure that we never give cause for complaint about the dogs we own. Although the beach is not an appropriate setting for every dog it can certainly be unusual and sometimes dramatic.

One problem that may be encountered is the direction of the sun. On a south facing beach in the northern hemisphere it will necessitate a picture against the light, if you are to include the sea in the picture. Don't forget the tide, because you may find the sea completely covering the sand at high tide. It is easy to make this mistake if you do not know the beach well; so consult the tide tables and avoid finding that a planned background no longer exists.

Temperament is another governing factor. Your dog must be off the lead – a dog on a lead by the sea fails to give an impression of happiness – but you will need to be in control of him. Your dog may feel that this is his big chance for a good run culminating in a dive into the sea. This could make a picture if he is not too far away but it will certainly make his coat wet which is most annoying if you intend a dry picture and have spent time preparing him. Dogs can become single-minded when they scent water. Rather like a field of sheep, it can attract a dog and make him amazingly deaf for the time being.

Holidays by the sea offer a keen photographer golden opportunities to employ his or her talents. Dogs 'on holiday' can make a picture book on their own. I saw an example during a holiday this year. Firstly there was a Jack Russell Terrier who adored sitting up in the front of a motor boat which eventually anchored in the bay a little way out from the beach, and then we saw a West Highland White Terrier hop adroitly from the rocks into the water and on to the shoulder of his owner, a handsome Frenchman, who swam with the dog out to the motor boat to visit the Jack Russell bitch and his friends on the boat. It all made a lovely sequence, but the problems of being prepared for beach photography were demonstrated by the fact that I had no camera with me for fear of it being stolen while we were swimming. To a dog owner who spends a lot of time on these outdoor pursuits my advice would be to consider one of the waterproof cameras designed to withstand rough handling and aim to have it available for the unexpected shot. Old dogs at the seaside and on holiday can be very appealing and I would simply try to portray them enjoying themselves with the family.

CHAPTER 5

Portraits

A close-up portrait of the head is probably one of the easier photographs to take and worth the trouble of careful planning. Ideally the dog should sit down to give a good line at the back of the neck and to keep him in one place so that the focusing can be more exact. To get a good angle the dog should sit facing slightly away from the camera, and

A German bred Weimaraner. I like the tones in the picture of this Weimaraner in the woods. The light had been so dull that I was forced to use a large aperture which gave me depth of field of only a few inches, but with a complete side view this was all the depth I needed.

Keeshond Ch. Neradmik Jupiter framed with heather and bracken makes a lovely picture. Such shots are never simple. It is easy with a panting dog on a bright day to get slitted eyes or too much tongue. Fill-in flash was used to lighten the shadows.

then to look over his shoulder towards you, or in the direction that seems best. This is really a tip from human portraiture where the subject sits in a way that diminishes the width of the shoulders – it is only for passport pictures or 'mug-shots' of criminals that the subject is photographed with the body completely face-on to the camera. The other advantage of the three-quarter pose is that the dog's hindquarters can be held if necessary to prevent him moving off. Naturally in some circumstances, as with pictures of people, you vary this – for example it could be unsuitable for a Bulldog where you might want to portray that solid look with the full power of the shoulders portrayed. Nor does it apply with puppies who should have that chubby, unsophisticated look that you sometimes get from a dog sitting four square on to the camera.

Technical problems of depth of field can spoil a portrait. A dog is a smaller than usual subject and photographs of the head alone can come into the realm of close-up photography, thus demanding special attention. It comes naturally to me to focus on the eyes as they are the easiest part of the head to see clearly in the viewfinder. This works well because, in order to achieve maximum sharpness over the whole head, one would focus approximately in that area, and also the eyes are the very part of the head on which you wish to direct attention. In bad light and in other conditions where you do not have much depth of field it is advisable not to take a photograph of the dog looking straight at you, but to turn his head to give a side view. Even a dog such as a Borzoi, with his extremely long nose, can be photographed satisfactorily at this angle as the depth of field needed is quite small.

Since this inability to achieve sufficient sharpness is one of the problems of dog portraiture, especially out of doors, I will explain it more fully. Depth of field is that distance between the points nearest to and furthest from the camera over which everything in the picture

Beware of laurel, or similar leaves, behind a very shiny or patchily marked dog.

Above – *The little Affenpinscher's wise, yet cheeky expression is the making of this picture, but without extra exposure for the black fur it could have been reduced to a black blob. The rather matt black of these dogs' coats make them susceptible to this problem, but this dog does stand out from the background although it is not completely contrasting.*

Left – *A similar picture has not worked well at all. The dog has lighter tones but the background, a nice bright green in the viewfinder, although out of focus, has proved to be a perfect match and quite an embarrassment to the photographer!*

Black and Tan Coonhound: Richlands's Merrie Maudella. Photographed in America, this bitch has a lovely soft expression and the plain background complements her colours.

appears to be sharp. It varies with the focal length of the lens, the distance on which the lens is focused, and the aperture in use. If the depth of field is very shallow then the dog's eyes may be in focus but his nose and ears may not. The closer the subject is to the lens, the shallower will be the depth of field. You cannot get round this by using a lens of longer focal length, to enable you to be further from the dog while still filling the frame, because the longer the focal length the less the depth of field. Nor can you use a shorter focal length lens to increase depth of field, because you then have to move in closer – and so you are back where you started! The way to increase the depth of field is to use a smaller aperture. But this will be feasible only if your shutter speed is going to be fast enough to stop any movement of the dog, and camera shake on your part. The smaller the aperture, the slower the shutter speed must be in order to give sufficient exposure. When I am facing this problem – with a black dog in dull light it can easily arise – I choose the small aperture and accept the slower speed, on the assumption that, on at least some of the shots, I will probably stop movement, but without a sufficiently small aperture the depth of field can never be enough. The answer to these problems is to use a faster film, but you need to assess the possible loss of quality against the gain in overall sharpness.

Having decided to feature the eyes, some breeds of the profusely coated kind may benefit from having their hair arranged so that the eyes will show well. A stray lock hiding an eye will spoil the shot, but

Ch. Ginger Xmas Carol. This Airedale bitch, Emma, was Best in Show at Crufts in 1986. I photographed her on the heathland near the lake where Tommy Gun swam and at one point she galloped off as if to do the same.

Make sure a lead does not show because it will spoil the picture completely (left and right). Hide the lead by turning the collar so that it is attached out of sight and then let it hang down behind the body to be held by someone behind, or in front of the dog, in such a way that it will be out of the picture (below left). Of course include only the area shown within the lines when taking the picture.

Right – For a portrait a dog can, if necessary, be held in position without the need for a lead. With one person holding on to the back of the dog another person attracts him, in this instance with cheese. The photographer moves in close for the shot and the helpers will be completely out of the picture. Care should be taken that the dog does not resent the restraint, nor prefer to pay more attention to the person holding him than to the cheese.

American, Canadian & English Champion Bibelots Tall Dark and Handsome. This famous Standard Poodle, known as Tramp, took the English show world by storm when he arrived from Canada in the 60s. His co-owner, Marilyn Willis, and I had great fun with his pictures, he was a real clown as I recall.

Left – *An Affenpinscher taken with my standard flash lighting set-up. My main light, in a large reflector, is beside the camera to my right, and the smaller light is on a stand to the left, slightly behind and above the dog. This second light kills any shadow from the main light and gives some highlight on the dog. The lighting is often revealed by the reflection in the dog's eyes, in this case the single front light can be seen. The white chair provides a fine background for this little dog.*

Above – *French Bulldogs have great character with all the fun, courage , beauty and charm of the more flamboyant breeds. There sad expression is only a façade!*

equally take care not to give your dog an unaccustomed expression. It is difficult to arrange coats exactly right, and some breeds can look all wrong if you reveal the eyes when they are intended to be hidden. Old English Sheepdogs are a typical example. Be certain that the eyes are clean and remain so, otherwise your portrait could be spoilt. It is a pity that light-coloured eyes are frowned upon in most breeds (even though the colour does not effect the dog's sight), because it is much easier to show the full expression in an eye that is not too dark. In any case it is always worth studying the eyes to make certain that they will not be in shadow and thus look rather blank. This can be deceptive and some breeds appear in photographs to have very shadowed eyes even when they have looked bright while the picture was being taken. I suggest you look carefully at your dog's pictures to see if you are getting this

Above – An expert coursing Whippet enjoying a comfortable rest on the sofa was photographed by the light from a window. New emulsions, with film speeds of ISO 3200 and higher, unheard of in the past, make it possible to use available light indoors with little difficulty.

Above Right – Basset Hound. This is the classic pose of the sad-faced Basset Hound and is not a difficult picture to take. Most dogs will not lie down in this way to order, although they will do so for hours when you are not ready with the camera. The lighting is not an example of my normal system; it will easily be seen that here I have used a lamp on either side and no back, or side light. The shadows are not obtrusive and the dog is well lit so this lighting is satisfactory and simple, though not adventurous.

Right – A perky Chihuahua.

problem. I have written quite a lot on fill-in flash in Chapter 8 and this can be used to good advantage here. Sometimes it seems not to suit a particular eye, and then a handkerchief or piece of tissue paper over

Left – This Afghan Hound comes from the famous Grandeur Kennels on Long Island, USA. Black easily goes too dark so I kept the dog in the sun and added fill-in flash to make sure of capturing all the detail, and the character in this lovely bitch's face. I also gave a little extra exposure for the black, which slightly over-exposed the background making it paler.

Above – Border Terrier American Champion Dickendall's Heart Breaker. The colours of the water, the charm of the terrier and the touch of fill-in flash combine to make this a picture.

the flash will soften the light if you find it looking too harsh. It very much depends on your own dog, but all-in-all I find fill-in flash effective and worth using.

Unlike in portraits of people, one of the fundamental questions in portraits of dogs is whether or not the sitter's mouth should be open. Dogs pant on a hot day or when excited, so there may be no choice, but some breeds look better than others with open mouths. Indeed with German Shepherd Dogs I sometimes specifically send a dog running about to warm him up so as to get a panting shot because this is one breed that looks its best open-mouthed, and is always photographed this way. Other breeds with similar head construction, the long-nosed dogs like Collies, Belgian Sheepdogs, and Afghan Hounds for example, also look attractive with their mouths open and showing some tongue. In the show world I am occasionally asked to photograph a dog with his mouth slightly open to give the impression of more strength of foreface.

Left – *A Clumber Spaniel. I took this picture while the dog was sitting in the ring at an outside show. Always trim the picture just at the back of the neck if the dog is on a lead, this concentrates the attention onto the dog's face. Soft, late afternoon sunshine avoided a harsh shadow on the unlit side of the head.*

Above – *Sh. Ch. Silbury Soames of Madavale. Best in Show at Crufts in 1964, this English Setter needed no special posing to look beautiful. The plain background of grass, thrown well out of focus, suits a pale coloured dog well.*

Left – *Samoyed Ch. Zamoyski Lucky Star of Ostyak. A special filter is used to form a star, but a patient dog is a necessity in a technically complicated shot.*

Above – *Ch. Alexandra of Daxlore. One of the famous Salukis in the history of the breed, this bitch was a genuine star. She loved the camera and was never happier than when posing for a picture.*

Those that should keep their mouths shut include the Pekingese, King Charles Spaniel, Bulldog, Pug, French Bulldog, Boston Terrier, in fact all those with shortish noses and wide deep muzzles. These breeds have distinctively shaped heads, some with wrinkling or flews, and an open mouth spoils the overall balance of the head, and if accompanied by a lolling tongue can be quite ugly. I have left out the Staffordshire Bull Terrier because they are specifically known as the laughing, or smiling dogs, and when they open their mouths and grin from ear to ear it can be most endearing.

Apart from these extremes, our dogs can be photographed as we perceive them looking attractive, but there is no doubt that if a bright, keen expression is sought then a closed mouth is best, whereas for a kindly, soft impression a slightly open mouth, with a little tongue showing, gives a friendly image.

Backgrounds for portraits are important but are generally quite easy to cope with. My bad mistakes demonstrate some areas that can trap an unwary photographer, but in the main it is a problem of merging and once this is sorted out a pleasant setting can usually be found. For some pictures, such as in a garden or the countryside with good plants to complement the dog, the background could be kept in sharp focus. Long grass and wild flowers are always lovely around a small dog. In contrast I have used plain painted walls, mostly grey or white, when there has been no other good choice, and they have looked remarkably good, and have given an impression of distant mist or grey cloud.

If the setting is not particularly good, it is better to resort to keeping everything behind the dog out of focus and turning it into a sweep of colour or a patchwork of tones. With my 150mm lens this is normal for a head study, as my illustrations show, but a lens of shorter focal length will give a sharper background necessitating a conscious decision to use a large aperture and careful focusing. Bear in mind that your dog need not always be placed close to a background, he can sit with space behind him and the effect can be studied in the viewfinder. An SLR camera, with its groundglass screen and a stop-down pre-view facility is very informative and will reveal any unwanted distractions which can be missed when the image is viewed at a wide-open aperture.

I will not go into the technicalities of artificial lighting indoors for portraits here since that is covered in detail in Chapter 13, except to suggest that instead of using flash, which may give red-eye, especially to older dogs, why not try some daylight portraits indoors using very fast film. Natural light is always pleasant and will reproduce the atmosphere of your home far more faithfully than flashlighting.

Portraits of little dogs may need provision for close-up photography. I have always used magnification (supplementary) lenses and have found them very good, easier than extension rings or bellows. These close-up lenses enable you to fill the frame and focus on subjects such as a toy-dog's head. Cameras without provision for accessories may not be any good for very small dogs so it is important to check this before you buy.

Effects filters can be fun, if you need effects. The one that gives an orange sky, in colour pictures, is sometimes quite good but it should not be used too often. I rather like the star filter but have only ever taken one dog with it. It is used indoors and you have to make a hole in the background paper and put a flash behind with its element directly behind the hole, because the star only works on a bright highlight. Other filters can be used to correct colour film as necessary, and in monochrome, yellow, orange and red filters are useful for darkening a blue sky.

Right – The famous Ch. Iceberg of Tavey could have been photographed from a slightly lower viewpoint to emphasise the feeling of strength, but by choosing a higher camera position the lawn only is behind the dog, with the darker line of shrubs kept above his head. Iceberg was on a lead, watching his rival in a tennis court, surrounded by high wire, behind me – an ideal set up which ensured the security of both dogs. Dangerous situations should never be risked with strong dogs such as Dobermanns.

CHAPTER 6

Viewpoints

One simple rule that many people know about photographing dogs is that the camera should be at the same height as the dog. This is quite right, but there are some considerations before making it a gospel truth and believing it to be the only way. With a telephoto lens the effect of a low or a high viewpoint is diminished, but the effect of a standard, or shorter focal length lens (50mm or 35mm) from a human's eye level can be disastrous. Distortion, which is mentioned in Chapter

15 on equipment, will give the dog the appearance of a large body and short legs. This should be avoided, unless you really intend to create a special type of shot, since distortion simply makes your dog look unattractive and unnatural. The best viewpoint for avoiding distortion,, if you are using a short focus lens, is from the side and at the dog's level.

I always go down, more or less, to the level of the dog, but my exact decision on the height of viewpoint when using my telephoto lens is often influenced by the background, which changes as the camera position is moved up and down. If there is a bad background that

Irish Setter. When taking a portrait there is a temptation always to choose a low viewpoint and a sky background, but it is worth looking carefully at your dog and deciding which angle you like best. I like the higher camera angle on the Setter which I think suits this particular dog, emphasising the soft and kind expression. I used a little fill-in flash because the shadows were rather harsh from a sun that was quite high in the sky.

Great Dane. In the case of the Dane the low viewpoint gives a feeling of strength and power. The black muzzle of the Dane must be well lit to prevent it going too dark.

would spoil my photograph I may have to sacrifice the best angle for the dog; an example would be where a black dog, photographed at its own level, would merge with a dark hedge. By choosing a higher camera position I would get the lawn behind the dog, with the hedge just above his head. It is a case of judging the importance of the pictorial element against the need to show canine excellence.

A low angle can be quite dramatic and it is used to help large dogs to look imposing. A big dog, such as an Irish Wolfhound or Great Dane, photographed from below can appear quite splendid and it is worth trying as a viewpoint for smaller dogs, especially if it will mean a better choice of scenery behind them. It is good for avoiding unwelcome objects on a distant background, such as a fence or house, which the low camera position will cut out, or at least diminish. However I think that low-angle shots can become too much of a habit and different views should be tried so as to get the best for each individual dog. Remember with head studies, that a low viewpoint gives a view of the dog from under the chin, especially if the lens is of short focal length and you are close to the dog, whereas a higher angle could well be more attractive for that particular head. A long focus lens allows you to experiment and decide upon the most photogenic angle for your dog, without fear of distortion. Ideally it should come naturally to study your dog in everyday life, from various angles, and to take note of his best expressions. If he puts his head on the ground when lying down, and gazes up, rolling his eye in the way a Basset Hound does, then this could be a good shot. But many dogs are not built to lie in this way and you might find a nice expression if he sits up and looks down on you. Your decisions should be based on your observations.

When photographing standing dogs in a typical show pose, the viewpoint is decided for you to some extent: there is THE way to do it

Saluki. With show dogs there is THE way to take many breeds. Mrs Hope Waters, the owner of this beautiful bitch has always liked unusual pictures but I thought this one might have gone too far towards the unorthodox as a photograph of a show dog – but she loved it.

Top Scottish Terrier Ch. Mayson Monopoly. Scotties are normally photographed slightly from the front, just how far forwards depending upon their length of back. Photography seems to lengthen a dog's back so this angle is used to counteract the effect and to give them the necessary compact look. This top winning dog would actually look good from any aspect but the svelte, alert, and balanced bearing of the dog is a credit to the owner and by no means easy to achieve. Black dogs are best photographed on a lawn that has a long sweep of uncluttered grass. The negatives should be slightly overdeveloped and a sufficiently hard grade of paper used in the printing to make the background white and to give detail in the black. If the dog is on a lead this can be dyed out on the negative so as to print white, and be lost in the white background.

Overleaf Left – Pembroke Corgi. If you stand your dog up in this way she may well stay long enough for a picture. Dogs seem to like this pose and will often look around keenly. Ch. Belroyd Lovebird is among the best dogs I have photographed for sweet expressions and her personality must shine through in the show ring because she is one of the breed's great winners.

Overleaf Right – A Boxer takes up the same pose on a convenient straw bale.

for some breeds. This may sound absurd, but it is based on the build of the breed and its most attractive angle. The long-bodied dogs like Corgis and Dachshunds are always taken from the side when standing, to avoid any possible foreshortening of the back. Length of back is all important.

Golden Retrievers, Labradors, English Springers, Irish Setters and other gundogs, hounds such as Borzois, Whippets, Greyhounds, Basset Hounds, also German Shepherd Dogs, Pyrenean Mountain Dogs, and some terriers with long backs such as Skye and Dandie Dinmont, are all breeds that are usually photographed from the side, with changes of angle to suit the dog's qualities or failings.

Very many breeds are taken from three-quarters front, and these are the dogs whose Standards ask for a compact shape. For some reason photography seems to lengthen backs, and sometimes a photograph from this angle will compensate for this and enhance balance and quality. For dogs with poor hind angulation (straight hind legs without sufficient bend at the hock) this is worth trying. Once you begin to notice such faults they can seem ugly and, if they denote a weakness, you feel the need not to emphasise them even if the subject is not a show dog.

The bull breeds are taken even more from the front: Bulldogs almost completely front view, showing their solid head and front, while Staffordshire Bull Terriers and French Bulldogs can have some hindquarter showing.

The photographer has such a choice in how he or she depicts a subject; we actually do not realise how many ways there are to take a picture. It is all according to our own appreciation of the dog in front of us. To go to extremes, a trendy photographer may feel the need to neglect all technical quality as long as the picture says 'DOG' to you. It does not matter in the least that it is out of focus, moved, and half the dog is cut off – Picasso is admired by some people and scorned by others. There is room for all styles and we can adopt old ones, or create our own, just as we wish. But for success in the conventional way of dog photography I think the real skill in photographing any breed is knowing to what extent you can depart from these principles on any particular dog and still show his virtues and type, without revealing any faults or ugliness. For example, if a dog of a short-backed breed excelled in this point you might take a full side view because this is the angle that really shows the construction of a dog who has no serious faults; the angle of the shoulder, the reach of neck, topline, set of the tail and hind angulation will all be revealed.

While it is not as important for a study of a pet dog, the slope of the ground on which the dog is standing must be watched. A dog's top line (the top of the back from the withers to the tail) in some breeds is sloping – everyone has seen the way a German Shepherd Dog stands –

in some breeds it is straight and level, in others it is roached, as in the Bedlington Terrier. Not only the top line, which is an important feature, but the whole balance of the dog can be thrown out of kilter when the dog stands downhill. Normally the best position is very slightly uphill, with the dog's front end a tiny bit higher than the tail end. I take a lot of Corgi pictures on a golf green with almost imperceptible slopes, and where I place a dog makes an amazing difference. For a serious photographer it is essential to develop an eye for the lie of the ground and the effect it can have. Of course if a dog is standing on uneven ground for a reason, for example he might pause on a rock climb or be contemplating digging up a molehill, that is a different aspect altogether. A dog can look very good with his front feet upon something like a straw bale or tree stump. They seem to hold this pose steadily and make an attractive picture, well worth trying for dogs of any shape or size. I am not certain why a dog likes this position, perhaps they have a better view of the countryside, but they often remain long enough for several shots to be taken.

I cannot abide fixed ideas that involve any sort of measurements being applied to a picture. Some people want to draw lines, such as from the shoulder through the elbow to the ground, or have the line from the hock to the ground vertical. I know that when judging dogs one may need these guidelines, but in a picture a dog should be seen as balanced and pleasant by eye and not with the ruler. This may sound inconsistent after writing about the way to take show dogs, but every picture should speak for itself and not be governed by preconceived rules that become an end in themselves. This applies to the animal itself and to that other great victim of measurement, composition. A wonderful picture may well follow rules, many of the old masters do, but I will not have a good picture condemned because it does not. A sports photographer's shot will rightly be allowed faults in composition, such as the horizon cutting the centre of the picture, and I think it is also a mistake to identify such errors in dog photographs. People seem to assume that a dog hangs around in his pose while we sit and study all aspects of the shot; this is so seldom the case – most good pictures are snatched.

I must mention the other prejudice I meet in my job of trying to take pictures that will please publishers, and this is a person's dislike of certain colours. I can understand that some brightly coloured indoor backgrounds are not always approved, but I have been asked on several occasions for pictures without certain colours, and these have included blue, brown, and even green in outdoor pictures!

The winning Pointer Sh. Ch. Pipeaway Scritti Politti on the Somerset levels. Photographed with no special angles or viewpoints – not pointing, not standing correctly, nor on flat ground. But a natural study where the ingredients are a beautiful dog, lovely background, fine weather and good luck!

CHAPTER 7

Backgrounds

Backgrounds can make or break a picture. In my early days, when my photography was mostly in black-and-white, some of my mistakes taught me lessons that have lasted a lifetime. They are still clear in my mind and, although I have not seen these pictures for years, it was easy to find the negatives from among my many thousands to illustrate these points. I remember that I was once asked for some wildlife photographs to demonstrate natural camouflage – the caption for one was to be 'animal invisible in grass', and this is the way to describe the

Labrador group at Chatsworth House in Derbyshire. A stately home is best kept in the background and not allowed to loom too large in the picture, otherwise it detracts from the dogs and is not itself seen at its best.

worst of them.   The trouble with these pictures, which were all for important commissions, was that the dogs were lost in the background, due to matching tones or too much clutter behind a dog that was itself parti-coloured.   Fortunately when taking colour any dangers of merging with the background are easier to perceive in the viewfinder, and failures are more often caused simply by the unsuitability of the setting.

Backgrounds are such a vital part of the picture, playing almost as important a part as the dog himself, but they tend to be completely neglected. Imagine a Stubbs painting with the dog standing in front of chicken wire and rubbish, yet this is so often the sort of place that people use for a picture of their own dog. The settings you choose should not only be free from obtrusive and ugly objects, but the picture will benefit if they are also in harmony both in colour and tone with the dog. The background should complement and embellish the dog, never

Left – *This photograph of a Dalmatian illustrates the need for care in choosing a background.*

Below – *The answer was found by taking the picture against the light where a similar hedge was in shade.*

Above Left – *John Holmes, the noted dog trainer, does not normally wear a Shetland pony on his hat!*

Above Right – *Avoid clumps of yellow or white in an otherwise dark border as these will invariably succeed in becoming an 'Ascot hat'.*

detract. I like to give the impression that the dog in my photograph lives a good life and that he spends his days enjoying green fields and the open countryside.

It does not take very much imagination to visualise the many mistakes that are made in the choice of backgrounds. Brick walls often appear in snapshots as do cars, bicycles, dustbins, washing lines and other such everyday items. The family dog may be used to sitting near these familiar objects, so their frequent appearance is due simply to inattention and photographing the dog wherever he happens to be. Of course if you have a wonderful new car or are very proud of your white laundry, the dog included in the picture will certainly enhance the shot – but leave them out when your dog is to be the centre of attention.

Among the good settings that anyone might choose are stately homes or castles. But it is a mistake to assume that because a place is known to be beautiful, it will automatically be good for a dog picture. I have even had it suggested that since a great house is full of works of art there is bound to be a good background in the gardens. When we chose a background for the book Champion Dogs of the World we decided to use Blenheim Palace, but we opted for the lake and bridge instead of the main house. Sometimes the posing of the dogs, without losing the beauty of the building or reducing the picture to a mess, can be difficult. It is often best to go some distance away to get the whole

Above – *Irish Water Spaniel at a lakeside. The blue water is obviously superb for this dog. I had photographed him in rather dull light a few days previously and had hoped to achieve a subtle effect similar to the Papillon on page 80, but in this case the pictures just looked drab. I retook this Spaniel in the sun and the colours of the water and the dog, as well as the stones and plants on the lakeside shore, make a good picture. The dog was a great character and, although he was trained as a gundog, his owner was not completely confident of his good behaviour at all times. I wanted him loose by the water for my pictures but there was always the danger that he would take a swim thus ending my pictures of him with a dry coat. The fleck of white on the water is the seeds from the plant growing on the right.*

Right – *A Saluki on a breakwater. A good example of keeping the camera ready and taking advantage of any picture that the dog presents you with. When out to photograph your dog, keep the camera set on the right exposure and ready all the time – a pose like this may only be held for a second.*

edifice in, and not just use the lower part of the walls, which may give no impression of the glories of the whole place. Going only a little way away may also give unfortunate 'hats' and extra ears caused by the arches and porticos behind the dog. People can stand anywhere and look all right, but it is not so with dogs. Ideally take the picture on, say, a hillside opposite looking slightly down on the building, thereby taking in the whole scene.

Left – Although a Rottweiler is black this dog's shiny coat has photographed quite light, so she merges with a background which is not sufficiently pale. The dark areas above and below the head are particularly distracting.

Below – A Maltese with two Norfolk Terriers – but one terrier has gained the ears of a Skye Terrier.

The relative size of any objects behind the dog will alter when lenses of different focal lengths are used. The perspective will change – the shorter the focal length of the lens the smaller the building will be, provided the dog is the same size in the frame – and so it is worth trying a long focus and a medium focal length lens – or whatever lens you own – and then studying the different effects you get. These shots work best for groups or big breeds, but if it is your dog and the picture is, in part, to remind you of a good day out then a stately home background is perfect.

Lakes and stretches of water are often chosen for a background and the smooth sweep of water can be very attractive. Water is never predictable in colour. It is possible to find even the Mediterranean Sea quite grey since the colour of water changes according to the colour of the sky. But other reflections too can give a great variety of shades and it is always worth taking advantage of any water where the colour suits your picture. Choppy water on a dull day can be bleak and colourless, so make a careful survey to check that it really looks good and do not use it just because it is known to be an attractive place. It may well be attractive only on a sunny day.

I always take the opportunity of photographing dogs against a blue sky at any time when the weather is fine. The colour complements any dog and is always pleasant to see, especially to those who live in a cold, grey climate. You can listen to forecasts and make plans, but there is no way of guaranteeing that the moment your dog takes up his pose there will be a good sky, and likewise when the skyscape is glorious there will often be no dog, no camera, or no time to take advantage of it. A dog in bright sun with a deep grey cloud background is always dramatic, 'the shaft of light' effect. This lighting is often used in painting but with animal photographs it is seldom achieved, for the same reasons that the cloudscapes elude us. Not so successful is a dog on a dull day, with no sun, against a pale sky; this seems to give a flared effect, especially with a dark dog, and I would always prefer to find a background with a light tone, such as a field, in these circumstances.

Probably easier to deal with are the more controllable situations, such as the garden or the local park, which are the places more often found when considering a good setting. There is always a temptation to place a dog in front of a flower bed, I have done it myself with my own snapshots at home, especially so when it is looking very colourful – but really the first consideration should be to find a place that does not compete, and one that will show off your dog.

Owners of the many breeds with pale bodies, but dark heads, may already have found they have a problem with finding a background where their dog's face will show up clearly. They will probably find that best results come from a background with a tone darker than the

Below – *Papillon standing on roots. Grey water can be bleak when used as a background, but in this case I saw that the colour of the water toned with that of the ground and I was able to make the best of the bad weather for an unusual background for this breed.*

Top Right – *Long Haired Dachshund Ch. Voryn's Cafe au Lait. I looked around an action packed garden for a background that would not overpower this lovely Dachshund. I found exactly the place I was seeking in a quiet corner – the plants and flowers give a simple tapestry effect, with the leaves only just out of focus, all complementing the strong shape of the dog. A colourful flowerbed is often chosen for a background, but an understated setting is often best, particularly with a richly coloured dog.*

Bottom Right – *Ch. Saxonsprings Hackensack. This Lhasa Apso was Best in Show at Crufts in1984. He stood beautifully for us on a cold and windy day on Ilkley Moor.*

body but not as dark as the head, possibly a long stretch of grass or far away hills. But stay clear of dark hedges or a line of trees at head height, or you will have a picture with the dog's face lost in the foliage. Tri-coloured (black, white and tan) dogs are easier than the black-faced dogs, because the face, which is so important, is not as easily lost in the background.

Black- or dark-coated dogs, of which there are many, need care in several ways and, of course, a pale scene must be found. But even here you must still use your eyes because the shine of some black dogs' coats may photograph quite light and not as the rich black you had expected. Black dogs against trees or a hedge are bad unless the foliage is very pale, but ordinary pale grass, hay fields and corn, are all good. This may seem obvious but it still has to be taken into consideration rather than trusting to luck, hoping for the best and being sorry afterwards.

White dogs, such as Bull Terriers, Samoyeds, Japanese Spitz, West Highland White Terriers, Pyrenean Mountain Dogs, and the cream coloured dogs, such as Golden Retrievers, Yellow Labradors, Norwegian Buhunds, are all a joy to photograph. They fit so well into our average garden or countryside and any areas of dark will just help them to stand out.

Having ensured that your dog will not be camouflaged you can now look at plants that could be used to good advantage. Surprisingly, stinging nettles always look nice in a background. Their dull, slightly patterned effect is attractive, but they must be out of focus and not really recognisable. Many other humble plants can be studied for their possibilities, yew trees, bracken, box and lavender are good. But not daisies on a lawn or flower beds planted in a dotted manner, or clumps of yellow or white in an otherwise dark border as I find that these will invariably succeed in becoming an 'Ascot hat' however hard one tries to keep them out of the picture. We are considering such plants as backgrounds well behind the dog but there are many that will look lovely close up or surrounding the dog, provided he is of a breed that suits that kind of treatment.

Views from hilltops of the surrounding countryside make an easy and undemanding background. They are beautiful to look at in themselves and are always successful. If you are planning to go to a certain place remember the sun's direction, as with the beach scenes, and be there at the right time of day for the light to flatter your dog. Ideally the sun should be behind you as you look out over the view, but of course this can be varied. It is most annoying to find a wonderful backdrop but be unable to use it because of the sun's direction. I have probably taken many successful pictures with side, or back light and it might be thought that the sun's direction is not important when one sees them. But there are always dogs that need the light to be directly on them, from the same direction as the camera, either because their dark coats, or their build, gives unattractive heavy shadows.

It is a mistake to think that all good background must be very beautiful to the eye; waste ground, quarries, piles of earth and ploughed fields can all be effective when out of focus and reduced to patches of tones. But I have found that very recognisable objects like a row of houses or a car will usually show up badly, and never go sufficiently unsharp to be lost.

As I mentioned in the section on buildings, photographic techniques can change the picture greatly. My photographs are mostly taken with a long focus lens (150mm on 6x6cm, format). As well as determining perspective, the backgrounds are rendered more out of focus than if they were taken with a standard focal length lens. I have no trouble at all in achieving an unsharp background and my style probably owes something to this. The normal way to prevent the background being too sharp is to use a larger aperture and so decrease the depth of field. This can be studied in the viewfinder by operating the pre-view button which closes down the aperture to the setting you have chosen. This is also useful for checking that objects that have disappeared in the viewfinder, through being completely out of focus, will not come clearly into view in the actual photograph when they are sharper. This problem is particularly well demonstrated with telegraph poles.

Dog photography in black-and-white needs a little more consideration and at times it pays to be cautious and selective. For example, a grey dog or brown mid-tone dog on a leafy green background may appear fine in colour, but even if out of focus the background may match the tones of the dog exactly in black-and-white. Beware, too, of laurel leaves and similar behind a very shiny or patchily marked dog. In a monochrome photograph a clear picture of a tri-coloured dog needs a plain mid-tone background to avoid losing any part of the dog. The black must not merge with a dark background, nor the white feet become indistinguishable in pale grass. With black-and-white photography it should be noted that an all-black, or an all-dark-brown dog can be made to stand out from a light background by contrasty printing. This will not work if there are dark areas in the background nor if the dog has lighter markings. There must be sufficient separation of tones between the background and the dog in the first place to be able to 'stretch' the contrast in this way. If the dog has brown on his legs (e.g. Dobermann or Manchester Terrier), this brown may go too light and the picture may not be successful. I have written more fully on this subject in Chapter 14 on darkrooms and printing.

Left – *Tibetan Terrier on a brown background. This picture illustrates that a good background does not have to be especially beautiful. This is a ploughed field in the flat counties of East Anglia. The touch of green, the pebbles in front and the proud pose of the dog all add to the picture.*

Above – *Labrador bitch with her puppy in the straw, a good setting for a bitch and puppy. We see so many plain green backgrounds that the golden straw gives something different. The winter sunshine, from a sun low in the sky, picks out the animals from the background and, while heavy shadows must be avoided in any important areas of the picture, in this case they are put to good use. I made a little set for this bitch and her puppies, the straw bales on either side kept the puppies in check.*

CHAPTER 8

Light and lighting

The quality of daylight plays an important rôle in producing an attractive picture, but perfectly good photographs can be taken in any light provided it is bright enough. I find that the film available to us today is very good at reproducing a dog's coat in a colourful and attractive manner, whatever the state of the cloud cover, but of course it is a good plan to recognise and take advantage of ideal conditions when they comes along.

My favourite light is hazy sun, it is a soft and subtle light which makes it easy to take pictures from any direction and it will light a dog well, giving texture to the coat and highlights in the eyes. I particularly like this diffused sunlight when it is accompanied by a touch of mist as this will provide a hazy, paler background which is excellent if you are photographing a dark dog, and could give you a pleasant high-key effect if your dog is light in colour. Do not make the mistake of thinking that yellow winter sunshine is soft just because it is weak. The low angle will bring many strong shadows and your dog will need to be carefully placed to avoid them.

On a dull day the posing of the dog to suit the direction of the light is much less important, and with black-and-white it certainly makes for an easier life, but as soon as the sun comes out one can see the extra dimension and enhanced pictorial qualities in the scene. It is interesting to note that many of Stubbs' dogs are lit with the soft directional light that one sees in the evening or at dawn when the sun is low in the sky. It is a perfect light (although the colour might be too warm for photography) but it is difficult to find in everyday life. Even on overcast days you should remember that the sun will still be there giving a directional light, although it may be imperceptible, and you can use this to give a slight highlight to the dog's coat, or to help pick him out from the background.

Some photographers dislike strong sun, but I think it makes the picture so much more cheerful that I seldom wish the sun to go in – unless the dog is suffering in the heat. In general I keep the sun behind me, in the old fashioned way, with as few heavy shadows as possible on the dog. Shadows are not flattering to the standing dog, especially when they fall behind the elbow and at the end of the ribcage, as they can make him look very thin and bony. In soft sunlight some shadow is all right as long as the dog is of a pale colour, but with dark dogs the shadows will very easily go too dark, the more so with transparency film.

At midsummer in some latitudes the sun will be directly overhead at midday, an unflattering light for anyone, as the top lighting will give heavy shadows on the dogs' sides. Follow Noel Coward's words and avoid the noonday sun in these latitudes – it will probably be too hot for the dog anyway.

Strong sunlight produces a bright, contrasty picture, but whether this will look too harsh will depend on the colour of the dog, its breed and shape, the angle of the lighting, the film used, the tone of the surroundings and the lens (some lenses give more contrast than others, regardless of focal length or the aperture used). A dog photographed near tall dark trees or shrubs, such as you find in some gardens or in a forest, will have much deeper shadows due to the lack of reflected light, though this may not appear to be so to the eye.

Using flash outside to lighten the shadows on a sunny day is known as 'fill in', and it is different from using flash outside as the chief source of light. A very small automatic flashgun is used, of just the right power to give the amount of light you need, in conjunction with the

Backlighting can be attractive. However, if you are photographing show dogs it is important that show points are not overlooked. The backlighting on these two Chows has made the coat translucent giving them the appearance of having very large ears. The correct outline is shown in the other picture where only the tips of the ears are seen.

Above – Dandie Dinmont portrait taken at a show in the USA. In spite of our best efforts this picture was becoming impossible to achieve. The wind was blowing strongly, shattering the bitch's immaculate hair. After we narrowly avoided being run over in the more sheltered car park, the owners suggested putting the dog on the trimming table outside their motorhome. It was mid-day sunshine and the dog's eye sockets were deeply shaded, so in desperation I switched on the fill-in flash and then took the shot while sitting on the ground beside the table to avoid a background of cars and vans.

Right – Bichon Frise in the corn. Even a white dog like this Bichon, Snoopy, in hazy sunshine would have too much shade on his face if I had not used fill-in flash. I like this picture now, but at the time of taking I gave up this place after a couple of shots because it did not look good through the viewfinder – the flash completely transformed it. Sometimes the ultra toy, pretty type of dog does not look right in a rugged landscape, but although this is a bit unreal, even the most coiffeured dog will act as rumbustiously as a rough terrier if given the chance.

aperture you wish to use. It is not difficult to achieve good results but you have to work it out. The big snag with a 35mm camera, which normally has a focal plane shutter, is that you cannot use a faster shutter speed than that recommended to synchronise with electronic flash (usually 1/125th sec, but faster with advanced systems), and this is rather slow for a sunny day.

With my Hasselblad, which has a Compur shutter synchronizing at all speeds, I use a flashgun which needs (for correct exposure as the only light source) a stop of about ƒ4 with ISO 100 film for a distance of

about 10 feet, or 3 metres. Using a stop of $f8$ to $f16$ (used with speeds of 1/125th or 1/250th) it works about right. Until everything is computer controlled this is the best I can do, as there are too many imponderables to be able to calculate exactly and still retain the flexibility and ease of fast shooting that is needed with dogs. Automation can fulfil your requirements exactly, but equally it may make it impossible for you to vary the way in which the equipment is used.

A reflector is usually used by fashion photographers working outside in the sun to lighten shadows, but although I have persevered, I find that they either blow away, frighten the dog or make him slit his eyes. Models' careers depend on their facing up to the glare of strong reflected light but dogs have no such ambitions.

Sunshine is very useful in providing a good dark background of deep shade either on the ground, at the bottom of a hedge, or beneath trees. Quite a small area of shade will suffice for a little dog and I use this quite often when I am photographing dogs such as small red terriers which, in black-and-white, can so easily merge into the grass. If the weather is really hot, take your dog into the shade for the picture. A dark dog can be placed so that the sunlit areas form the background, they will be quite burnt out, and thus white, when you expose correctly for the dog. The lighting on the dog in the shade will be very flat, but not unattractive. Some dogs with large beautiful eyes may not be able to keep them open in strong sunlight and much of their charm will be lost, so try them in the shade or turn their backs to the sun, using backlighting. This will stop the dog squinting and prevent the eyes from running.

I have not discussed backlight very much because I do not use it a great deal. This may be because the majority of my subjects are darker in colour and therefore the unlit side of the dog has to be lightened by flash or reflector. On paler dogs there is always the danger that the top of the head or the nose may be burnt out, losing all detail, and thus losing the dog's expression. Humans when backlit will have their hair burnt out and this would not matter, in fact it could enhance the picture. This of course is a generalisation and not a fundamental rule of dog photography, for backlighting is one of the first experiments a budding photographer will make in the quest for more interesting pictures. Having said, and believed, that this is not my favourite light, I am surprised to find how many of my pictures in cloudy, but bright, conditions are backlit, and to good effect. I use backlighting more often when I am photographing with colour negative film since it is less contrasty than transparency film and the whole effect is softer.

With show dogs there is always the need to pay due regard to the points applicable to the different breeds. For example, back lighting can take away some of the substance from a dog, especially if the highlit hair merges with the background; I have found that backlit

Sunshine is very useful for providing a good dark background of deep shade, either on the ground, at the bottom of a hedge, or beneath trees. Quite a small area of shade will accommodate a little dog and I use this quite often when I am photographing dogs such as small red terriers which, in black and white, can so easily merge into the grass.

pictures are rarely chosen by owners, even though they have been superior pictorially. The Spitz breeds, and other dogs with small ears partially hidden in the coat, (for example Samoyeds, Chows, Pomeranians), should not be taken with the sun behind them, because the light shines through the coat on the head showing up the full size of the ears and making them appear too big. This is immaterial to the pet owner but for pedigree dogs it is important.

The colour and quality of sunlight varies throughout the year. In winter, and towards sunrise and sunset, the light is yellower than at midday in the summer. The animal photographer has enough to contend with without worrying unduly about this and anyway may want to use a late warm sunlight for a pleasant evening effect. But it is worth knowing what colour a dog should be, and whether or not it is important. Dog colours are not merely a modern whim of fashion, but depend a lot on history and tradition. Colours are in some cases important to help distinguish one breed from another. It is interesting that so many white dogs are allowed, according to their Standards, to have markings of another colour, or are permitted to be less than 100% white – these include the Maltese (may have light lemon markings), the Samoyed (can be pure white, white and biscuit, or cream), and the Pyrenean Mountain Dog (patches of badger, wolf-grey or pale yellow allowed). Quite a lot specify jet black and this means black and not brown, so ideally one would not photograph a black poodle in evening light. Sometimes the liver colour is essential as with the Irish Water Spaniel, (it should be so-called puce-liver), while the Sussex Spaniel is a golden liver. Several other breeds specify that liver is objectionable so it's a colour to watch. Irish Terrier may be bright red, red wheaten or yellow red. Norfolk Terriers, often noted as being red, may also be all shades of wheaten as well as black and tan. Some breeds surprise us by the number of different colours that are permissible – Chows are not only red, but also black, fawn, blue, cream or white. Scottish Terriers are black, wheaten, or brindle of any colour. Many Standards, however, say that colour is only of no importance within reason (for example white Boxers or German Shepherd Dogs are quite beyond the pale, although some people prize these colours when they do turn up). So I think that it is true to say that since there are no flesh tones to worry about – no faces to take on blue, green or orange tones – the exact colour of most of the dogs in our pictures does not matter too much, and in this we have an advantage.

CHAPTER 9

Puppies

The photographing of puppies can be completely maddening and absolutely delightful at the same time. However naughty the puppy, you can never really feel cross with him and as long as you work hard and keep your patience you will, with luck, get a good picture eventually.

Maltese family. The last litter of the famous Vicbrita Maltese kennel and a work of art in preparation and presentation. These are active dogs who, like babies or small children, will get into a mess if they possibly can, so a picture like this is not easily achieved. I was fortunate that the sofa and matching cushion made a good background, and also that its owner was prepared to risk it to the possible ravages of puppies. My diffused flash lamp was fairly high to my right. The other lamp, high towards the back on the left, as well as providing highlights, has cut the shadow cast by the little puppy at the front, but was too far back to obliterate the shadows on the back of the sofa. This is unimportant with white dogs on a dark background, but it would need attention if the dogs had been dark on a light ground.

Left – *Mastiff and puppy. Another of my old pictures that we all liked. The favourite dog, Withybush Crispin, and his daughter, of Miss Bell, an old-time Mastiff breeder. A picture like this is much more easily taken in black and white because any small faults can be corrected later in the retouching or finishing.*

Below – *Maltese puppy. A magazine wanted photographs of this beautiful white puppy playing outside in the mud. 'NO' said her owner firmly, but the pile of leaves made a good substitute.*

Left – *Otterhound and puppy in the USA. Otterhounds are wonderful dogs. Those I have met seem to feel the need for a gallop of a few miles between shots. However they love to pose for the camera in a light-hearted sort of way. They have special ears that hang in a fold and their attention must not be attracted for they lose their Otterhound look when their ears are not completely dropped. On the day I took this picture the weather was dull and wet, I had very little depth of field and was using a slow shutter speed so, rather than chase the dogs around for action shots, I took carefully posed pictures beside the lake. Although the water is not colourful the muted tones suit the picture well.*

Above – *Old English Sheepdog. The black patch on the puppy must be kept clear of the dark background for obvious reasons.*

The easiest age for really appealing pictures is around 6-7 weeks, especially if the mother and puppies are being photographed together as a group. At this young age the pups have just begun to look like real dogs, and they are generally more malleable and less mischievous than you can expect them to be later. They also tire more easily, at least before you do, which may not be the case when they are older.

Unfortunately a puppy does not normally leave the breeder to come to his new home until he is at least eight weeks old, and this is just about the time he has found his feet and is learning the joys of life. So although you will have missed the earlier peaceful stage, now is the time he will be at his most photogenic and you should be prepared and ready for action as soon as the puppy is with you and has settled down. Bear in mind that he will quickly grow up, and will suddenly be at the leggy and sometimes plain stage, beginning to lose his puppy coat and the special charm that all very young animals have. Although this new stage will still be a good time for pictures, they will not be 'the day you could hold him in the palm of your hand' type of shot that will bring back such happy memories of floor cloths and disinfectant in the years to come, when your dog is a staid gentleman or peace-loving old lady.

As with photographing adult dogs it is important to have time enough to exercise your patience and good organisation to ensure that you will not be interrupted. Try to get help from an agile friend, because the job of fetching and carrying is the donkeywork of puppy photography – and never lose your optimism about the possibility of a good shot.

Before beginning the session I make up my mind as to the type of picture I intend; either I will follow the puppy around outside and take the photograph when he looks good, or I will choose a certain place for a completely posed picture. Usually if I am working indoors my lighting will allow only the latter.

The secret of good posing is for the subject to look normal and

A rather old-fashioned, longer-legged Chihuahua with a puppy.

Toy Poodle puppy. Show Poodle puppies stay in a special puppy clip until they reach the age of one year, then, shorn of their puppy coats, they go into the adult classes with the sculptured lion, or similar clip. Many times I have photographed Poodle puppies and telephoned through to the owner to confirm that the pictures were OK and that they could go ahead and clip the dog. If your dog is to have a radically different trim, for any reason, remember to take a picture of 'before' and 'after'. A light coloured dog is easy to photograph on a dark background in this way.

natural; the puppy will be best in a comfortable place like his basket. I do not like pictures where the poor dog is perched up on a high place or crammed into something, it is the dog you are photographing being himself, not being forced into a situation. Of course, there is a time and a place for that type of cute, posed picture, but it is very difficult to do well and often just looks silly. If done successfully you have the somewhat old-fashioned 'table-top' style that was the norm years ago in dog photography. It is still popular for chocolate boxes, but for pictures today I prefer a more realistic style.

Back to the puppy, I would always rather take the pictures outside and follow the dog about, provided there is somewhere safe and photogenic for him to go. This it is not necessarily the easiest way since you must attend to the exposure constantly and watch the changing light and background, but there is more scope for an interesting and unexpected shot and, most importantly for me, there is a chance for the puppy to take up a pose himself, giving a picture that portrays his character better than would a static indoor shot.

Finding a background inside the house for a puppy is easier than for an adult dog, because you need only a small space, but you are unlikely

Right – Golden Retriever and puppy. I had not paid much attention to this picture until it was chosen for the cover of Das Tier. A single puppy with a bitch is often more effective, and much easier, than the whole litter. This picture has no exciting backgrounds or special lighting, it relies entirely on the positions and expressions of the bitch and puppy.

Below – Bulldog bitch and puppy. The same applies to this picture.

to have chosen your furnishings to match the dog and may well find that nowhere is suitable. When your puppy and furniture do suit each other a sofa or chair is a good place to position him but take great care that the puppy is in no danger of falling to the ground and being hurt.

You must avoid the appearance of your dog sitting on a chair that has been covered with a dust sheet – nothing looks worse than a sheet or curtain draped over a chair. I was tempted to try this when I first began as it seemed an easy way out, but it always looked a mess and the pictures were never satisfactory. For a little puppy I find a length of material that complements his colour, paler rather than darker and the heavier the better. Place it over the back of the sofa so that it runs forwards smoothly over the seat. The puppy can sit in the middle of this and it will give a sweep of colour all around, but be careful the edges do not show and ruin the illusion. (He may also ruin more than

Golden Retriever bitch in whelping box. It is lovely to have a picture of one's bitch with her puppies but all too often there is so much work to be done that photography is forgotten until it is too late and the birds have flown the nest. Make a plan as to how the picture will be before the birth, then it will be easier to put into practice. My first shot shows the whole scene – albeit tidied up – of a whelping box with all the necessary bits and pieces.

A simple tranformation which gives a better view of the dogs themselves. A different litter but a similar scene – the front of the whelping box is removed and a washable white blanket, which I use for puppy shots, is spread over the box to give a plain background. Usually it is wise to allow the bitch to stay on her normal home ground to be certain that she is not upset in any way. Lighting may be difficult as whelping boxes are normally in small rooms. I used my main light near the camera, but not too close to the dogs. My second light was high up near the far wall, shining into the box as far as possible. Exposure is difficult to measure as the scene is so pale, therefore this would be an occasion for bracketing (taking several shots at different settings) assuming that your subject is remaining reasonably stationary for once. If your bitch and puppies are black then a blanket background that is not white might be better. The glare of the white can make the photography of a black subject more difficult and any light colour would be better.

the illusion if he is a youngster, so a towel and plastic sheet beneath the cloth is a good precaution). Needless to say, if your rooms are full of lovely things your pup can sit among them, but it should look sensible that the puppy is there. I like to distinguish between a picture which is intended as a study or portrait of the dog, and one which is illustrating a moment in the pup's life.

'Colorama' paper is specially made for photographic backgrounds and comes in many colours. It makes an excellent sweep of background, but it must be used with care. Firstly, it is easy for a dog to step

Australian Cattle Dog puppies. In a different style are these tough little Australian Cattle Dog puppies in their box in the stable. These dogs thrive on the outdoor life and, full of mischief, are much more easily photographed when contained. We had worked out that six weeks old would be a good age for photography but these pups were so advanced that they had reached their hooligan stage two weeks early. There was only room for one light in these circumstances and my diffused flash worked well considering the difficulties.

backwards into the paper and, unless the roll is securely suspended it could come down on him. Secondly, the paper makes a thundering noise when moved which can be frightening to a young puppy.

Maybe you wish to send a photograph to your puppy's breeder for assessment of his show prospects, or simply to show how well he is doing. Many people just take a sitting picture, but the breeder would much rather see the dog standing side view so that his development and general conformation can be seen. You will certainly have to stand behind the puppy holding his head and tail, but do not worry if it is not an artistic picture, you can take others that show the happy life he is leading.

All good owners will bring up their puppy nicely and start elementary training, but it is often the naughty things that are so appealing, so spare the rod while photography is in progress, indulge your subject and keep him happy.

With a big group I would hope to have, if possible, a bitch who is controllable and will stay in position as the centrepiece. If there is no bitch, then decide on one pup who is to be the anchorman – the most amenable, or tired, so your selection may change as the session goes on. A helper on either side fields the puppies and returns them to the anchor dog, holding the little bodies as necessary and letting go at the right moment. In this way you can start with one or two in the picture, and slowly build up to the complete litter. It usually takes about 45 minutes for the pups to tire. Be patient – do not shout and row – impossible though it will seem, they will settle eventually and go sound asleep in glorious photogenic heaps, just when you have had enough and have shot too much film anyway. Needless to say, if the dogs are in any way upset or the bitch growling you should not attempt a picture. A word of warning here, do not tempt the puppies with food, otherwise

American Cocker Spaniels. Sh. Ch. & Am. & Can. Ch. Hu-Mar's Hellzapoppin at Sundust, known as Carlos with one of his puppies. Fill-in flash lights the shadows.

there will be constant pauses to clean up the background, which will slowly become plastered with the bits that are dropped or missed. A bitch with very young puppies can be bribed with little bits of biscuit – drop them among the pups and she will take an extra special interest in her babies.

Try to use equipment with which you feel comfortable, otherwise you will have all the normal problems of dog photography but more so. A puppy is a very small thing and likely to whizz about giving you no assistance at all, therefore your technique must be very slick, and when working indoors your lighting must be simple. It would be quite possible to build a little set in which the puppy could be contained but since I always try to take puppies in their own homes it is not practicable to make very elaborate arrangements that may not work anyway. One breeder I know photographs her puppies over the top of a low-sided outside run, sitting with a telephoto lens waiting for the dogs to pose themselves. Very good results can be achieved like this, but ideally the run should be built of some attractive material or disguised in some way to avoid a wire background.

All-in-all I think it is the will to win which is the important factor; some people give up before they have begun.

CHAPTER 10

Action

Dogs are really exciting subjects for action pictures and improvements in camera design are making great shots all the easier to take. When Muybridge discovered over 100 years ago, through photography, exactly how a horse's legs move at the gallop it was quite revolutionary. I know that it may not surprise the nation to see a picture of your dog moving at high speed, but a sharp picture, showing every detail, will be fascinating to you. The long-haired breeds are those that one would visualise to be great action subjects, since their flowing coats will provide the artistic element, but the smooth coated breeds are just as rewarding if the rippling muscles and power in the dog's limbs are caught in sharp focus. The corded breeds can be quite spectacular in movement, and a fully coated Komondor on the move or jumping is an amazing sight.

Besides the straight-forward shots of galloping or playing, your dog may also be a worker – he may be trained for agility, obedience, retrieving, pointing, digging, or water trials. You might even have a guide dog in the family, or your Bloodhound might be a member of a local pack. All these activities are excellent prospects for photography.

Agility

This is the up-and-coming sport for dogs, it is great fun to watch and I imagine exciting to take part in. The dogs negotiate a series of obstacles, such as jumps, tubes, and see-saws. They should present little problem for pictures, because you know exactly where the dog is going and you can practise panning and focusing on the right spot in advance. There are many good moments in 'Agility'. I particularly love the way the Border Collies seem to hang in the air as they fly over the jumps, clearing them by a huge margin.

At Crufts the Agility Event is a big attraction and takes place, as do the other classes, under artificial light. Normally a film balanced for tungsten (ordinary electric) light should be used because a daylight film will show a marked warm or brownish tone, but it is variable when television lights are used, and for perfect results further enquiries

Afghan Hound Ch. Viscount Grant Best in Show Crufts 1987. Taken with an auto-focus camera and automatic exposure, but not motordrive. The dog is nicely centred and the auto-focus has worked well. A zoom lens of 75-150mm was used as the dog obligingly circled us in his gallops. He is an exceptional Afghan Hound, the breed is not renowned for their qualities of obedience, but his owner Chris Amoo, and the dog understood each other and although this was taken in a big city park there was no danger of Gable, as he is known, running away. Afghan Hounds at the height of their show careers must preserve the long hair on their ears which cannot be allowed to become tangled, so they wear a sort of dog's hairnet while exercising. I try never to ask for too much when owners pose their dogs for me, so I was grateful to Chris Amoo for the time he gave me and hope that no harm came to Gable's beautiful ears.

should be made as to the exact colour of the lights. Blueish filters can be used to convert daylight film to tungsten light, or slightly blue filters for use with photoflood light, but they will necessitate extra exposure which you really cannot afford when the level of light is low. Using negative print film you could take a chance on daylight film and have the colour corrected in the printing. Alternatively you can just accept the colour change which will not be disastrous. It is not unusual to see illustrations reproduced in books where the wrong film has obviously been used. For black-and-white there is no problem, except for the low level of light. Use a fast film and in some cases it may be worth up-rating the film speed, (under-exposing), and arranging for special processing. Otherwise, if the light is only sufficient to give you a slow shutter speed, try very careful panning which sometimes gives interesting results, or photograph the dog on the table where he has to 'Wait' for five seconds. You can use flash, if it is permitted, but only if you are within range. It is no good expecting a small flash to light a dog in the ring if you are sitting several rows back. For show dog owners who may want to photograph their dog in the Group it is probably best to use the available lighting and steady the camera on a support. (I will not suggest that you bring a tripod, that would be the quickest way I know to have him beaten in the breed classes!) But a support, such as a monopod, could be useful in these conditions to avoid camera shake. People and dogs are usually reasonably still in the Group, so if the camera is stable you can use speeds down to 1/15th sec. Fast film speeds of ISO 3200 make black-and-white photography possible in very many more situations than could be attempted previously and indoor action shots are often well within reach.

Komondor in action.

Above Left – *A moving subject requires a fast shutter speed to stop the action. This is normally used in conjunction with panning the camera in the same direction as the movement. In this picture the dog is sharp.*
Above Right – *insufficient shutter speed was given, and no panning, which has left the dog blurred.*

Above Left – *A picture with correct shutter speed.*
Above Right – *shows correct panning but too slow a shutter speed, the middle of the dog is sharp but due to the rotary motion of the dog's head and hindquarters there has been considerable blurring.*

Retrieving

'Retrieving' pictures need a little thought. A dog carrying a bird is an attractive sight, but in an action shot you must catch the dog at the right moment. As he brings the bird in he should look balanced – the weight of the bird in his mouth may cause him to move awkwardly – and he should have a good grip, picturewise, on the bird. Although dead, the bird has to look pleasant, its legs or wings should not hang in an ungainly way. A portrait of a good-looking gundog holding a game

Newfoundland at water trials. The patient dog was completely at home sitting in his wet boat waiting, one might imagine, for someone to rescue. These water trials give the chance for wonderful pictures if luck is with you. The darkness of the dogs' coat makes carefully judged exposure important because the brilliance of the water will infuence the meter and give underexposed blacks. This picture was taken on a dull day, the negatives were given extra developement, and the print was on paper sufficiently hard to give detail in the dog's face and body.

Pointer on point. For this shot the owners and I drove 250 miles to the moorland where the Pointer had received his training. We had previously bought a pheasant from an expensive London shop and tried to set up a pointing picture in a field nearer home, but the dog, instead of pointing, walked up to the bird and lifted his leg on it!

bird is a traditional picture and even those against shooting will admire the bird's beauty, the wonderful colours of the feathers and the gentle expression on the face of the dog.

I find that many people involved with working gundogs keep an unplucked bird in the freezer so that a picture can be arranged at any time of year. The trouble is that birds have shooting seasons so really your background must comply with this if it is to look authentic. If you resort to a frozen bird remember to defrost it so that it hangs correctly in the dog's mouth.

If you are not keen on shooting, good pictures can be taken of a dog going through all the actions but using a training dummy.

Pointing

The actual photography of a dog on point is simple. The difficulty may arise when the dog will not point to order, nor in the right place for

Long Haired Weimaraner. If you can be certain of the exact spot from which your dog will take off you can pre-focus and then concentrate on panning and getting the right moment when he jumps. This dog has made a lovely graceful curve as he jumps into the blue water which shows his distinctive colour well. The first shot is always important as in the next one the dog will be wet.

your camera. A professional gamekeeper may have some creatures on which he trains his dog to point and a picture can be set up, but if you are hoping to feature your own dog it is more exciting to go to a moor where the dog will point naturally. Great energy may be called for as the dog always seems to scent the game far away – then lose it, only to move off again just as you reach him. I have spent many happy hours trying to catch up with Pointers who rejoice in bounding about in deep heather while I make much heavier weather of it. Dogs on point do not always take up an attractive pose – they do not necessarily strike the attitude that you find in paintings – but a trained dog can be manoeuvred without difficulty into a good stance. A dog on point is somewhat transfixed while he continues to scent the quarry, so you do have an opportunity to compose your picture. I would just advise lightweight equipment if you plan a few hours running around on the moors – but it will be very beautiful especially if the weather is good. It is a lovely way to spend the day.

Digging

Digging is the natural pursuit of terriers but unfortunately it is bottoms up while they work, so a little manipulation is necessary for a good photograph. You can choose either a big hole to put the dog in, and have him looking round at the camera, or the terrier can be just emerging from the hole – more or less a head and shoulders shot with background. Both are effective. While out walking it is worth looking

Above – *Border Collie working sheep taken during rehersals for the TV programme* One Man and His Dog *where I was taking stills of 'behind the scenes' activities for the book of the series. Even in my good position I was still unable to get a really good shot of the Collie 'eyeing' the sheep, but this picture shows him turning the sheep towards me. In the printing I 'held back' the background over the dog so that he stands out from the dark trees behind.*

Below – *After the trials the shepherd returned the sheep to their home pasture. His bitch, Tess, moved the sheep up and down the field for my pictures, in the sun, but this unplanned shot was the best.*

Above – *Large Munsterlander retrieves a pigeon – but it is obvious, from the the bird's shape, that unfortunately the dog can only have retrieved it from a deep freeze.*

Below – *Norfolk Terrier swimming on Dartmoor. Swimming dogs are easy to photograph because their actions are predictable.*

Above – *Ch. Montravia Tommy Gun is a great Standard Poodle, he won Best in Show at Crufts with his owner Marita Gibbs and the last thing I expected when I went to photograph him, was the chance of pictures in the water. I had used the Gibbs family's garden as a background before but this time Tommy Gun had spotted a pet rabbit and his aim, above all else, was to find it. There was no chance at all of his standing still in the garden so Frensham common, a local beauty spot, was decided upon as an alternative. It was a very hot day and, after the main pictures, Tommy Gun was given a swim in the lake. I was astonished because a poodle's coat is sacred, but I followed him into the water and got some thrilling shots that have since been published on book covers and in magazines around the world. But disaster nearly spoilt our efforts, the processors had a fault in their machine and one batch of my film came out purple. I have learnt that things will go wrong in photography if they possibly can, so my safeguard is never to have every film from one job processed at the same time, thus I never lose everything of one dog. Only two rolls were lost of Tommy Gun – but it was bad enough.*

Top Right – *Newfoundlands at water trials.*

Right – *A Border Collie, Queen, working ducks.*

Miniature Poodles from the Montfleuri kennels enjoying themselves.

for photogenic places for a digging shot, bearing in mind the direction of the sun and the best time for attempting a picture. A problem is often a low level of light, as suitable holes are usually under trees. A group of small terriers in these woodland places makes a lovely shot but it is hard to pose and you need luck on your side.

Water Trials

Water Trials are held for Newfoundlands because their natural skill is to work in water, and this includes the saving of drowning people. It is very amusing for the spectators to watch a supposedly drowning owner imploring her dog to come and rescue her – to no avail. But the trials take place as a fun activity without too much formality and can be good to photograph. If you intend to take some serious pictures I advise talking to the organisers first, and arranging for everything to be as photogenic as possible – wet-suits and other gear should all be in good condition. Those who really have influence could try to get the trials staged so that the action will not be against the light. Newfoundlands are very dark dogs and back-lit shots are not ideal. As well as saving drowning people, they will take the tow rope of a boat in their mouths and swim, drawing the boat to the shore. These kind, sweet-faced dogs seem really at home in the water or in a boat and are most photogenic – as long as you get the detail in the black and do not lose the expression in the face.

Swimming

Not only Newfoundlands but all dogs are good to photograph in the water. The movements of swimming are predictable and methodical and therefore easy to catch, but the dog will be within range for only a short time and you cannot afford to be slow and miss a picture. Be prepared, and, as with all action, do not sit around and wonder if your exposure and focus are right – work everything out in advance. Although the swimming is slow and peaceful, before his swim a dog either jumps or splashes into the water and photographing that can test your skill. The fastest shutter speeds are needed for the jump. If you can pre-focus on the point of take-off, then only a little depth of field is needed so you can use a large aperture, (thus allowing a faster shutter speed). If, however, you expect the dog to dash about and jump where and when he feels like it, then more depth of field will be required to allow for faulty focusing. A balance will then have to be found between shutter speed and aperture in order to stop the movement and achieve enough depth of field. In my experience many shots will be unsharp through movement or lack of focus unless the light is very good and fast film is used. The dog will probably be jumping in after a stick, or similar object, so make sure it is thrown accurately in the direction you wish. Concentration and observation will be rewarded in these shots. Remember that the dog will not go on jumping for you forever – he and your stick thrower will become tired of it, so try not to miss any chances. If your dog is a spectacular jumper then you should catch him looking marvellous as he sails through the air, but any dog looks good as he dives into the water. Make sure you include the water in the picture so that it is quite clear where he is jumping. There is a 'wrong moment' and that is just as he is about to touch the water, but before he breaks the surface. This 'walking on the water' can be amusing, but equally it can look strange as the water could look more like ice since your fast shutter speed will have frozen any movement of the water. The next good moment is as the spray comes up but just before he goes right under – a fraction late and you will have only a big splash. A motor-drive can be used for all these shots. It may help you catch the right moment and a sequence is always nice, but bear in mind that if you have failed to focus correctly or there are any other errors you will not cure them with a motor. In a sequence of pictures the dog should, ideally, move from left to right as this looks more natural than vice versa when you look at the series of prints together. Polarizing filters are sometimes recommended for eliminating reflections when photographing animals in water, but I have never owned such a filter or found the need for one.

Guide Dogs

A guide dog is so very much part of the family that a photograph of him will always be treasured by the owner's friends and relations. Although

Tibetan Terrier

the owner is unable to see the picture he may well want one to show friends. A family with a guide dog does not need me to tell them this, so my suggestions are really for people like myself, who are outside the family and may be taking some pictures to give to the owner. As well as guiding shots try to get some informal ones of the dog with his owner. Theirs will be such a special relationship and with an animal as well trained and intelligent as a guide dog any picture should be possible.

Sheepdog Trials

Sheepdog trials are always extremely difficult to photograph. A photographer is not normally allowed close to the action for fear of distracting the dogs, so one has to be content with dots in the distance while the dogs are working. If you do not want to photograph the dog while he is actually competing the best way is to pose the pictures after the dog's run and hope you can beg some sheep for him to work. You will want to catch the way the Border Collie 'eyes' the sheep, but it is not easy to arrange things so that you see both the collie's face and that of the sheep. It is simple to get the dog looking into the camera with the sheep behind him, but this is totally wrong and will be obviously so to anyone who knows about sheepdogs.

A sheepdog on his own is not difficult because, like the Pointer, he can become transfixed when working. He will move slowly up to the sheep, given the correct commands, and you can position yourself between the dog and the sheep, getting the full benefit of his 'eye'. A Collie working ducks in water is also a wonderful sight and makes a superb picture.

Border Collies are usually black and white, and a small amount of flash is useful to lighten the black in a close shot of the face. You cannot simply give extra exposure for the black, because this would overexpose the white of the dog, and the sheep, if they are included, and the background.

If you have a long telephoto lens, sheepdog trials are among the few

Yorkshire Terrier jumping. Top winning Yorkshire Terrier Ch. Yadnum Regal Fare enjoys himself with a tremendous leap for my picture. A fast shutter speed assures one of more success, in general, than trying for artistic blur. My exposure time of 500th second has not stopped the movement on Regie's head, although the coat on his hindquarters is sharp.

opportunities for photographing a dog doing something on his own. Most dog pictures necessitate some posing, setting up, and controlling of the dog, but with sheepdog trials you become more of a sports photographer, which to me has great attractions.

Hunting

My experience of fox hunting photography is 'they went thataway'. Go to the meet – and then go home and sit by the fire! But there is more to hunting than Foxhounds. The advantage of a day out with a Bloodhound pack is that you know exactly where the hunt will go because the quarry is man. A willing chap runs the course, and waits at the end for the hounds and riders to track him down. All very good sport, and good pictures too, particularly when the hounds find their man – no blood, just furiously wagging tails and much licking of faces. Draghounds, similarly, run on a previously marked-out course and there are none of the frustrations of foxhunting, but Draghounds are, however, rewarded with chunks of meat at the end.

Playing

One of the most difficult shots is of two dogs playing. It is easier if they are young puppies and play all day, because after a little observation you can judge their next moves, but older dogs may have to be prompted and tend to play their best games when you least expect it. Adult dogs may play well at tug-of-war but they are unpredictable and will probably give up just when you have got yourself organised. With any playing shots great agility is needed to get into the right place for the picture. For example if two dogs tug on a cloth or hold a stick they will wheel round, necessitating a quick dash to a new camera position. Innocuous swear words may well have to be devised to ease the pain of so many good pictures missed. A single dog with a toy, stick or bone can produce a masterpiece. The picture should concentrate all the attention on the dog's sparkling, mischievous eyes if it is to be a close-up, alternatively it can be a full action shot showing the animal having fun.

Shots of a lone dog running round after a person seldom work well because the human legs always seem to get in the picture. But a dog who gallops around on his own for the pleasure of it and within photographing distance is perfect, provided your eyes are sharp if you are focusing manually.

This chapter has not, so far, been concerned with technicalities, but there are several points worth mentioning. Action photography is often a welcome change and the results can be most rewarding, but like most worthwhile photography it needs some forethought. Panning (moving the camera as you take the picture) in the same direction as the action helps to achieve sharpness in the moving dog and also blurs the background. Although this is much easier than one would imagine, it is not as simple with dogs as with some other subjects. The secret is to be quite sure of the actual direction of the movement you are panning with; a galloping dog will be going slightly up and down; a dog scaling a jump will go up, stay still momentarily at the top and then come down; a playing dog will be all over the place. In addition to the body movement the legs will also be going in all directions, and so it is all the more difficult to get a picture where the dog is sharp throughout. A fast shutter speed is, of course, required to freeze the action of a

Guide Dog with his owner. It is not difficult to photograph a Guide Dog taking his owner skilfully round the hazards in the street, but in this case I wanted informal pictures of them together.

moving subject, but sometimes it is fun to use a slow shutter speed to get a bit of blur and to give an increased feeling of movement. You could choose a shutter speed of 1/30 or 1/60 sec. and pan with the movement, but even slower speeds can be tried. This technique is not something to be used all the time because there are so many failed shots. It should be remembered that the thin line between masterpiece and rubbish is sometimes unclear, but it is always worth giving any sort of picture a try to establish whether or not it is for you. Take a lot in the hope of one great shot. I have always found that blur is all too easy, even with a fast speed, and in general it is sharpness that I seek.

Action pictures can sometimes be enhanced by using a little flash at 'fill in' strength. It will help arrest the movement, and it will not give you a double image – at least not an unpleasant one – if your panning is good and the shutter speed 1/250 sec., or faster. In fact I like the pleasant effect of slightly blurred coat, combined with some that is pin sharp through the high speed of the flash. A weak flash may also light up the eyes which, if you are fortunate, can add a great deal to the photograph. The flash must not be strong enough to act as a main light, otherwise the picture will appear to have been taken at night since the background will not be lit. There are techniques of using flash with daylight, exposing for it as the main light. Combined with a slow shutter speed this gives a sharp dog on a very blurred background. These action pictures are interesting to take because, although with the right camera you have complete control, there is no way to be certain of success. Exposure calculations for fill-in flash can be complicated, but many modern cameras with automatic exposure programs offer the facility of combining flash with daylight. If you want to know more on the subject of flash with daylight for particular automatic cameras I suggest you buy a book on your camera or look out for articles in photographic magazines where this seems to be a favourite subject.

Flash with a fast shutter speed requires the type of shutter that is not found on SLR 35mm cameras. They have focal plane shutters which generally only synchronise with flash at speeds up to 1/90 or 1/125 sec, or sometimes 1/250 sec. Leaf or Compur shutters allow synchronisation at all speeds and are generally found in 2 1/4" square (6 x 6) cameras, including the Hasselblad and twin-lens Rolleiflex. Some compact cameras also have shutters allowing synchronisation at high speeds. Anyone wanting to use flash with fast shutter speeds should check carefully that the shutter on the camera will synchronise.

Another problem that needs consideration is focus. To obtain a picture of a galloping dog a good way to simplify the focusing is to get him to run from one person to another over a particular spot on which you pre-focus. This can be marked with something natural like a flower or stick on the ground which will not show up in the picture but will enable you to pre-focus and the helpers to keep the dog moving over the right spot.

The modern autofocus camera should simplify all types of action picture and enable even the most ham-fisted photographer to get exciting results, but I will give a few words of warning, aimed at enthusiastic amateurs who might have become adept at using an old friend of a camera and feel they would like to change to autofocus. The autofocus lens will focus on whatever is in the very centre of the picture; if your dog is to one side of the frame, the background will be sharp but not the dog, although with some autofocus cameras you can focus on the dog and lock the focus.   I would advise against using autofocus for photographing a dog jumping an obstacle because if your dog is not exactly in the centre spot as you pan with the movement, the system may well send your focus onto the background. It is better to pre-focus manually on the jump, and your focus will be correct when the dog arrives. Without the option of manual focus, for example with a compact camera, you must keep the dog as large as possible in the viewfinder and risk cutting off his feet or tail as the dog jumps – take several shots to give yourself more chance of success. Some advanced autofocus systems are able to keep track of a moving subject and detect the direction of movement, so read the manual on your particular camera carefully.

A motor-drive helps with action, enabling you to take a series of pictures in quick succession. It should be possible with all this automation to follow a dog as he runs around, the zoom lens keeping the dog filling the frame, the focus correct, the exposure taken care of automatically, and the right moments, with luck, captured by the motor-drive or built-in camera motor. Good results can be achieved – with luck on your side there is always the chance of an amazing picture.

CHAPTER 11

Dogs with children

The photography of children has much in common with that of dogs so there is little need for me to talk about the technicalities. Recording confrontations between dog and child can, however, be likened to photographing two express trains passing each other, there will be only one moment of exposure where the whole dramatic effect is portrayed.

In many ways it is difficult to know exactly what to recommend about taking pictures of one's own children with the dog because it is such a personal matter. Have the camera around and take a picture as one occurs – this is the way it has always happened in our family. Speedy reactions and quick picture composition are essential ingredients in either posed or informal situations. The similarity to Press photography can be appreciated because, out of the many shots taken, there may be only one that justifies all the time and effort.

During the different phases of childhood one's method for obtaining pictures must change. With a baby it will depend completely on how the dog is integrated into the family as to whether the two can be photographed together. A picture of this nature is of necessity formally posed, as the baby generally will tend not to react to the animal, but when the baby is older they may begin to play together. It is essential, of course, that care is taken with regard to the baby's safety.

Toddlers in my experience must generally be crept up on. Little children and dogs are naturals together, but co-operation you cannot expect. A long focus lens will be very useful as one is really taking a candid-camera type of shot and any obvious interest shown by you in the subjects will almost certainly result in an end of activity by the child. It is a case of 'softly softly catchee monkey'. Even at a later age of six or seven there will be a tendency for children to over-act if they see that they are the centre of interest and so the same approach should be taken. The dog of course will be oblivious to anything outside his immediate attention, but no move should be taken to get him to look at the camera. You have to accept that the two subjects are doing their own thing and interacting, so be patient and wait for the shot to appear. This is easier said than done as you could be waiting a long time, but one must remember that there is double the opportunity of missing a superb shot if you have two subjects, so be constantly aware of what is going on through the viewfinder and do not be afraid to shoot.

When your child is older there will be a more reasoned reaction to the taking of photographs so a more formal pose can be undertaken although, as we all know, there might be a bit of petulance. A small dog can be held in the child's arms while you take portrait shots. It is acceptable with this type of picture to attract the dog, but the human

A posed shot and although it is a nice picture there is not the spontaneity as shown in the picture with the baby on page 31. The boy is showing evident pleasure but the puppy is not so sure. A typical pose of a young boy who is completely at home with his equally tough puppy. This dog enjoys a bit of rough and tumble and a 'soft' picture brimming over with affection would not be appropriate.

This little girl was watching me photograph her bigger brother with another dog and wanted to participate. Her mother let her hold this puppy which she immediately took for a walk and I was able to take this charming picture, but it had to be quickly done as in a few more steps she would have been up-sun necessitating a change to the settings on my Hasselblad. With an automatic camera this would have caused little or no problem.

half of the picture must cooperate and maintain a photogenic pose until the shot is finished. With bigger dogs, of course, this type of pose is not possible and you may be faced with a dog that wants to run around if off the lead, so you must devise a scene. You can consider having the dog on the lead and under control, but if you wish a more informal picture the child will have to keep the animal by his or her side, possibly with the aid of food – but the food should be dry and clean – biscuits and cheese are useful; this will ensure that the dog does not become bedraggled around the face and spoil the picture. It does however depend on your dog's fondness for food as you do not want it to

Getting the subjects together can be difficult, especially with puppies, so get the child to hold the dog – if the right size – and take a portrait. This photograph was taken at the end of a session but the soft evening light has given a very nice tonal quality. It is worth attempting a shot in these light conditions as so often if it is successful a pleasant result can be obtained. Fill in flash is not recommended as this would give a complete change in the picture with the subjects brightly lit and the background darker giving an unbalanced look.

become obsessed with looking for titbits. I have found with this sort of setup that the dog tends to stand with its back towards you gazing up at the child's face. It is essential that if this happens the child manoeuvres the animal into a satisfactory position whilst maintaining a stance facing the camera. After all, you do want to have faces in your picture. It is also possible for another adult to stand alongside placing the dog in position and stepping smartly out of the picture, thereby overcoming this problem. But, as you can see, it is essential that your child really enters into the spirit of the day and helps as much as possible.

Action photography is a must. As we have all seen, family dogs react to children and this does make this type of picture more feasible. An active dog will run and chase with the children so this activity can be used to advantage. Do not expect a dog to behave differently from normal. Be aware if the animal tends to get hysterical with a ball, or that it loves to chase cats. Do not let a situation arise where such factors can come into play. Know your dog and the same of course applies to the child. When photographing your own family and animals all likes and dislikes will be known and consequently it is unlikely that any session will get out of hand.

If the dog likes a ball or maybe a squeaky toy the child can control the action to a large degree. Keep them to a certain spot or small area and good pictures can be obtained by manoeuvering the object of the dog's desire to bring it into a good position. Perhaps the dog likes jumping up, if so get the child to spin around encouraging it to jump in the right place for the camera to catch the mood. Another nice, but simple picture is to ask the child to run along an agreed line with the dog alongside or at heel. One can pre-set the focus and pan with the child. But be sure that you are sufficiently in control of the child that he or she will do as you ask. Children can be contrary!

With teenagers one really does find that photographic work takes on a new meaning. They usually have insufficient patience with adult behaviour and any attempts to take pictures of them with the family dog will be an insufferable bore, consequently time available is generally short. A set-up posed shot needs to be well thought out beforehand and taken with as little fuss as possible. On the other hand, as I have mentioned before, holiday times can be more acceptable to the subject and a bit more cooperation will be forthcoming. Again it is essential to be quick as the subject may indulge in the popular trick of making faces at the camera if boredom is allowed to creep in. Of course with a young child this can be quite humorous, but annoying where a nice portrait is wanted for the family album.

It is worthwhile having a record of child and dog through the different ages. Why not consider this. It is fascinating to look back over the years and see the development, not only of your child, but of the dog as well. It is surely a much more worthwhile subject than all of those landscape views which, unless of a special place, mean nothing after an interval of years. With these pictures of the children and dogs memories flood back and can give endless pleasure.

Although I have specifically given this chapter over to children and dogs the same principles apply if you wish to photograph other members of the family, using the dog as a prop to make a more natural picture. In such instances the human half of the photograph will have a better understanding of what you need and consequently more attention can be given to posing the dog.

In my work I often have to borrow children and dogs for a picture and find that after about 9 or 10 years old the children will pose very well as long as they are fond of dogs and they are old enough to treat the session as work. It is generally better if the parents are not there as the child will usually work better without them, especially if given something to do. But, although they will do as you ask, it is very hard to get a child to play with a dog to order, or to act completely as if the dog were their own much loved companion. I am of course particularly careful in my choice of dog, trying to use those that I know well, contacting all the aquaintances that I have made over the years to find just the right one for the particular job. It is absolutely essential to get an animal that is of even temperament and is known to like children. Even under these circumstances the dog should not undergo endless pushing and pulling about.

All the foregoing relates to outdoor photography but if indoor flash work is being considered the control necessary becomes even more rigid. It is better to refer to those chapters on lighting for the technical side, but I would only say on the modelling requirements that both the child and dog come under a stricter discipline which can result in an unrelaxed pose. If the models are sitting on something make sure that it is safe for both dog and child and not likely to prove unstable. Remember that an average sized sitting dog requires more space from front to rear than a sitting child, as otherwise you will waste time and shots as the dog scrabbles for a firm base. A small dog, such as a Chihuahua or Pug can be held on the lap, but on the other hand a dog like a Great Dane could be much taller than the child. Overcome this problem by sitting the dog on the floor with the child standing alongside to start with, and then experiment to see the other, more interesting poses that may be forthcoming.

These differences in size can be used to good advantage to create impact or a theme – such as a big dog being the protector with a small child. An older child with a dog and you have the reverse, the child looking after the dog – or a boy and terrier 'me and my chum', a bit sentimental perhaps but certainly worthwhile to get a really charming picture.

Above – *With a potentially difficult group like this you rely on the cooperation of the child which, at this age, one should expect. In this case I reminded the girl to look happy, not anxious, while I concentrated on getting the right moment for the animals.*

Top Right – *My son was sitting with the puppy talking to his friend and for once I managed to produce the camera without his knowledge and got this shot. Both subjects are unaware of my interest and are concentrating on the immediate point of attention.*

Bottom Right – *In this posed shot I have chosen a low camera angle to ensure that the child's face would be visible. From a standing position only the top of her head would have been seen.*

CHAPTER 12

Films and exposure

With black-and-white work, on 2 1/4" square (6 x 6cms), I have always used a fast film (with a normal developer), and have found the advantages so great that I seldom use anything else. Slower films are often recommended because of their finer grain, but I have found that my prints have been satisfactory even for big enlargements. On the rare occasion on which I use 35mm monochrome film I do choose a slower, finer grain film where possible, because a 35mm negative must be of good quality to be certain that it will enlarge well. Coarse grain is admired as an art form at times, but I feel that this treatment in general does not suit dogs.

The majority of my colour work is on transparency (slide) film, and many of my pictures that are currently published were taken in the days of High Speed Ektachrome of ISO 200. This film was excellent but it changed in character and colour and, after a few years of trying various makes, I now use Fujichrome ISO 100 which is actually too slow for real comfort but has brilliant colour. Of necessity I do so much photography in dull light, often of drab-coloured dogs, that any brightening of the tones that the film imparts are very welcome. Muted colours can be lovely, but regrettably so much is lost or changed in reproduction that working to get subtle effects is often a waste of time.

I like the Fujichrome ISO 400 film very much, but find the ISO 100 preferable for everyday use. I strongly advise trying out fast films to see how far it is possible to go without losing quality. The ISO 1000 film has, so far, been too grainy and not pleasant for dogs but no doubt this will change in time, making life so much easier. When I want prints only, I use colour negative film and find it really beautiful and so much easier than taking transparencies, but for my work for publication I have to use transparency film.

When automatic exposure metering first came in many professionals felt that such innovations were not for them, but with dog photography the more help you can get the better, and I do welcome it on my 35mm camera where it works extremely well. It may be that with the greater latitude of colour negative films and accurate automatic metering the problem of getting the exposure right has lost some of its terrors, but for thoughtful photography it is good to have some knowledge of the technicalities and how they apply particularly to the problems of dogs.

The difficulties for us lie in the extremes of tone we find in dogs' coats, in other words the white is so white, and the black is so black. The rule is that dark dogs must be given more exposure, mid-tone dogs are normal, and white dogs need less. This is the simple principle I grew up with, and it was so easy to put into practice on my box camera with all-manual settings. Today's automation, with the array of metering modes, both helps and hinders us.

It is well known that the background influences a meter reading but, for the time being, I am leaving out that aspect and concentrating solely on the actual dogs. All the mid-tone dogs such as Irish Setters, Airedales, Finnish Spitz, the darker Golden Retrievers, Hungarian Vizslas, Yorkshire Terriers and Bulldogs are beautiful to photograph in colour – exposure presents no problem. Also the red and white dogs like Welsh Springer Spaniels, Red and White Irish Setters, Cavaliers and King Charles Spaniels of these colours, and Wire and Smooth Fox Terriers make a good picture without too much trouble. Weimaraners are fascinating with their luminous grey coats which can come out light or dark with all the subtle shades in between. With all these dogs you can simply take a reading on the dog and the exposure will be right.

But dogs with dark faces and light-coloured bodies can be really difficult, Afghan Hounds with pale gold bodies and dark masks are typical of this problem, as are Bull Mastiffs, Pugs, Great Danes, Pekingese, Cairn Terriers, and Briards that have this darkening round the muzzle to a greater or lesser degree.

When photographing a dog of this colouring I would suggest increasing the exposure by about a half stop and, if possible, reflecting some light into the face by putting the dog beside a white wall or sitting him on light-coloured gravel or paving stones, or by water – anything that will throw up some light. These dogs are particularly badly affected when the background is pale and automatic metering is used. A combination of this and the dog's light body colour will persuade the camera to give a correct exposure for the dog's body but allow the dog's face to go too dark. A more complicated answer (though simple on a camera with this facility built in) is to use a small 'fill-in' flash on the camera, but it must be balanced with the daylight and not too strong (see Chapter 8). Arrange for the flash to give about a quarter of the recommended exposure for the flash, i.e. 2 stops underexposed. This relatively weak amount of flash will not normally give a red-eye effect, although I once had another version of it, 'yellow eye' on a brown Newfoundland.

White dogs can also be tricky and must be given less exposure, anything up to a stop, depending on film being used. But in strong sunlight care must be taken not to darken the shadows too much when decreasing the exposure for the white coat. This is especially applicable towards the end of the day or in winter when shadows are more pronounced. Again this is most noticeable with transparency film.

Black dogs need more exposure, and in black-and-white more development (see Chapter 14). There seems to be a general belief that you cannot take a good picture of a black dog but this, of course, is not so and given the right treatment they can photograph well. The dogs with very textured coats of matt black need particular attention, these include black versions of Pekingese, Chows, Schipperkes, Affenpinschers, Giant Schnauzers, Scottish Terriers, Pulis and Poodles. All these dark dogs need care in poor light, especially in portraiture where there is not much background and the dog's features alone are making the picture.

Dark liver- or chocolate-coloured dogs like Irish Water Spaniels, Sussex and English Springer Spaniels, Newfoundlands and brown Poodles sometimes photograph very dark, particularly on dull days. It is well worth noting that these tones can be treacherous and may come out much darker than they seem. But I like the sort of halo around the edge of a dog of this colour that shows up against a darkish background, when there is only a slight trace of backlight, giving a very pleasant effect.

Dobermanns, Rottweilers, Pinschers and Manchester Terriers photograph well because the tan on their faces provides enough lightness to bring detail into the face, and their build and coat texture seem to be photogenic. Flat Coated Retrievers and black Labradors can be very shiny in the sun and will need some extra exposure – but do not give too much in bright weather because the bright shine of the coat can come out quite light.

When I say 'increase or decrease the exposure' this means that it should be changed from the exposure that the meter indicates for an average scene. If your camera is not automatic, simply open up by half a stop or a stop according to the darkness of your dogs, or stop down similarly if he is light. A camera with automatic metering will make adjustments through its metering system. But the extent to which it will take into account the dog's tone depends on the amount of the frame he is filling, on the brightness of the background, and on the nature of the camera's metering system – centre weighted, spot, multi-zone, for example.

This is a bit of a minefield because of the variables, and there are no definite rules on how to solve this exposure problem, (apart from the grey card system). I have said that white or black dogs need adjustments to the exposure but in practice if you use an automatic meter, a dog reasonably filling the frame would be correctly exposed provided that a black dog is well lit without shadows. But because this is not based on sound photographic principles it could fail you in some circumstances. For example, when there is a lot of background to influence the meter it will not take the reading predominantly from the dog and can cause a black or a white dog to be under- or overexposed. Unfortunately it is possible for the automatic metering to react to extremes of the black or white of a dog's coat too much, and when it is critical (as with transparency film) it may actually be necessary to give more exposure on a white dog and less on a black one to counteract the camera's over-enthusiasm – all a bit of a conundrum.

Many pages can be written about exposure metering and there are cameras with different modes to enable you to take readings from different segments of the picture – but I cannot see this working for dogs who will not occupy the same area of the picture for long. Experienced photographers will be able to decide how best they cope with extremes of black and white, and beginners to photography should experiment if they own a dog of difficult colouring – based on the over- or underexposure mentioned above. If your dog comes out too dark, on the print or transparency, he is under-exposed, if too light he is over-exposed.

The correct way technically to establish exposure is to take a reading on a special grey card (such as the Kodak grey card available from photographic dealers) held in front of the subject, towards the camera, and then to judge the exposure according to the reading and tone of the dog. With my Hasselblad I use a prism viewfinder with a built-in exposure meter. It is not automatic and the reading has to be transferred to the camera manually. When photographing an animal with very light or dark colouring, or a contrasting background, I take a reading on the grass in front of the dog (similar in tone to a grey card) and make a judgement from that. It is quite possible when using a camera with a viewfinder display to do the same, so as to see the difference between the reading on the mid-tone grass and the actual subject, thus establishing the increase or decrease in exposure that the system has measured.

Adjusting the exposure when it is automatic is done in different ways. To be able to alter a compact camera you must have a plus or minus setting. More sophisticated cameras will have a control to set up to three stops difference either way. It may also be possible to change the exposure by altering the film speed setting (when there is one). I prefer not to do it this way because it is more easily forgotten and left incorrectly set when not required. To understand fully how a meter works I recommend Ansel Adams' book The Negative – metering is quite a technical subject and it is well worth understanding the principles.

If you are are worried about the correct exposure when taking colour, you can bracket the exposure. To bracket is to use different settings for successive pictures, usually a half-stop apart, so that at least one of them will be correct. It is a technique beloved by many people, but is normally not done with action or animal photographs. We cannot risk a great shot being one of those incorrectly exposed so should try to get it right every time. My only exception is if the dog is completely steady and stationary then I might take five or six frames on the estimated correct setting and, if the dog were still there, I would then take a few over- and under-exposed.

Another much acclaimed device for automatic cameras is the Exposure Lock which enables you to keep a button pressed to 'hold' an exposure reading taken on one subject for use on another. This is rather tiresome with animals because you have to wait too long for the right moment and would be far too hampered with one finger kept pressing a button. Remember that too much fiddling can lose the picture – tests and experience of photography of your own dog are really the best answer.

The reflected light from the snow has helped to lighten the shadows and dark face of this Bullmastiff puppy. However great care must be taken with meter readings in snow since the brightness can influence the reading resulting in under-exposure of the dog's face.

CHAPTER 13

Indoor lighting

Through my family connections with our fashion studio I have had access to many lighting systems, but I still like my extremely simple and most effective electronic flash set-up. It is true that custom built, sophisticated, continually up-dated flash equipment is very nice, but I have photographed animals with complicated lighting arrangements, designed for fashion or portraits, and found it can be quite unsuitable.

Left – *Italian Greyhounds. A example of bad flash lighting with the shadows everywhere. This is a difficult picture to light, but a main light, fairly high at the front, sending the shadow down behind the dogs, and a second light of less power placed quite high up from the side and fairly far back, picking up highlights would be better.*

Right – *A neat portrait of a Cocker Spaniel. A diffused light in a large reflector from the left and slightly above the camera is used with a second lamp near the background.*

I take most of my indoor pictures with two lamps: one is the main light in a very large reflector with the actual bulb capped (this gives a soft light similar to a flash directed into an umbrella), the other light is in a fairly small reflector, giving a harsher light. Maximum output of the main light is double that of of the small light, but the actual strength is somewhat modified by the different reflectors, and both can be used on full or half power. This second lamp is an enormous improvement on just a single light source and, as long as you are not photographing a large group, it is all that is required to photograph a small subject like a dog. I use a third lamp when a large or distant background has to be lit, such as a room setting where the whole scene must be shown; in this case the third lamp lights only the background.

I position the main light as close to the camera as possible and slightly above it, according to the exact lighting I want. By keeping the lamp close to the camera the dog's shadow on the background falls down behind the dog, and it can be partially killed by the second light. Because of the large size of the reflector the actual flash is always a foot or more away from the lens and so there is no possibility of getting red-eye. The second light is placed high, and quite close to the background, on the opposite side from the main light, giving some highlight on the subject while also lighting the background. I always stay close to my main light – if I move my camera position the light must go with me because otherwise I will be photographing areas of the dog that are unlit. It must not be thought that one lamp can bathe the dog with light when viewed from any angle. I find that a dog's face needs to have plenty of light directly from the front to avoid strong pockets of shadow, which occur far more easily than on a human face – the darker the dog the more this applies. In portraiture of people the main light is normally set up to one side and the shadows are filled in with a light on the opposite side. This gives good modelling, and is undeniably a nice light, but a dog is different, he does not have a nose like ours, the coat does not need this treatment and lighting for him should not really be based on human portraiture.

I see many animal shots, not only of dogs, where a light has been placed on each side resulting in the sides of the animal being well lit but with unpleasant dark shadowy areas at the front, the very part of the animal, the eyes and nose, which most need to be emphasised.

For lighting to appear natural there should only be one shadow, or at least only one definite shadow cast by the dog on the ground or surface he is placed upon. When you photograph the whole body of a standing or a sitting dog there will be two shadows if a light on each side is used. This is a point specific to dog photographs because in human portraiture the feet are seldom included. It looks particularly bad when a dog has very thin legs, such as a whippet. A footballer under floodlights casts four shadows from the lights at each corner of

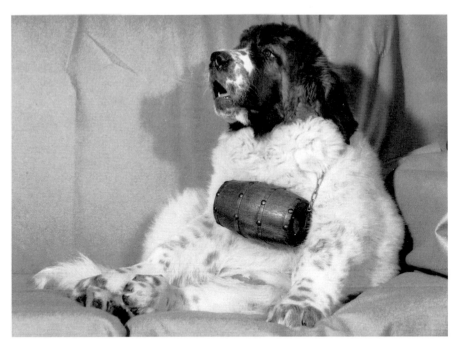

Above – *An example of a good subject ruined by bad lighting and a poor background. The felt background is good in itself but should have been ironed and arranged far more carefully on the sofa. The dog is lit by two simple flash heads, one on either side of the puppy, as can be seen clearly by the shadows. I took this picture many years ago before I had got my act together on lighting and have regretted ever since that I did not make a better job of it.*

the ground and demonstrates the odd-looking results of having multiple light sources.

Dogs are extremely variable in shape, so the snub-nosed, round-faced Pug could reasonably be given different treatment from the long, slim, aristocratic-featured Borzoi. Even so I feel the trend today is towards simplicity, and though the lighting I have described generally suits my style, whatever the dog, it can easily be altered if a moody or atmospheric shot is wanted. Another reason for using my particular set-up is that the dog will often move around and may get too close to the main light (if it is to one side), thereby ruining not only your exposure calculations but also the balance of the lighting. This can happen easily with a group of puppies. The behaviour of dogs is unpredictable, and a photographic session with lights can easily become chaotic, so the last thing you want is a complex lighting arrangement adding to your troubles.

A practical point to be considered is that usually an anxious owner is standing close to the dog to control him, and there is just not room for a light on each side. Inexperienced people, as well as getting in front of a lamp, will also be inclined to step back and send lights crashing down – so will boisterous dogs. With my system the photographer can hang on to one lamp in a crisis and the second lamp is reasonably out of the way. Fashion and portrait photographers can use overhead boom lights but I hesitate to create any possibly dangerous situations and also must watch that puppies do not chew the cables, so I have as few hazards as possible.

The type of lights used for this work often have a modelling lamp, (to enable you to see the effect of the lighting the flash will be giving). Full use should be made of this to ascertain where the shadows will fall and also to assess the balance of the lighting. You will not want to waste any time fiddling with the lights when the dog is on the set so use an object about the same size as the dog as a guide, adjusting the lights to your satisfaction. Remember that the further your model is from the background the lower the main light shadow will fall on the background. The modelling lamps can be left on while you are photographing as they are a help in focusing when there is insufficient light to see your subject clearly. Do not, however, overheat your dog as light bulbs give out quite a lot of heat; on a cold day this could be used to advantage and it has been known to encourage the family cat the join the picture. It is important to remember that the room lighting, or the daylight in the room, will not light the picture, (unless you especially intend it to and expose for it) so do not be deceived by any brightness which will not reproduce in the picture.

I use a flash meter to determine the exposure. With flash you only need to know the aperture because the speed is simply that of the flash. You must just set the correct shutter speed to get synchronisation of shutter and flash. A reading is taken by pointing the meter at the camera from just in front of the dog. I take care that the side light is not influencing it too much, but equally I do not screen it completely from the meter. I also use the flash meter to check that both lamps are giving about the same reading, or to within a stop (this will give balanced lighting), pointing the meter at each light source from close to the subject. Having taken the reading it may then be necessary to adjust the aperture according to the tone of the subject. A dark dog will need up to one stop more exposure, a white dog one stop less.

Many flash guns are computerised and will give you correct exposure automatically. Or rather one hopes, and believes so, having read the advertising. But the flash gun's computed exposure can be incorrect in the same way that an exposure meter can get it wrong for a black or a white dog.

To summarise – using a flash meter you measure the light falling on the dog and adjust the aperture if your dog is of extreme tones. A computerised, automatic flash will vary its output according to the tone of the dog, but may still not give a correct exposure. A simplistic explanation goes like this – the amount of light reflected from the subject is measured by the flash gun's computer, with a black dog it thinks 'this is dark – I must pile on more light'. It does not realise that this is a black Labrador, and meant to be black, consequently it can give too much light thus overexposing the dog. It can also be incorrect when a part of the picture is light, the computer may react to, and expose for this light area and thus underexpose the rest of the picture. It is for this reason that professional photographers, when faced with difficult subjects, make their own calculations rather than relying on automation.

For users of non-automatic flash set-ups another means of determining exposure is through the Guide Number system. These are quoted by the makers to denote the flash strength, but for greater accuracy are best worked out yourself with a series of test exposures. The Guide Number is the distance from flash to subject (in metres or feet, with a given flash and a given film speed) multiplied by the stop. If the correct stop is $f8$ at 4 metres then the GN is 32. Although a Guide Number is simplicity itself it is sometimes written as GN 32m ISO 100 which can sound a bit forbidding but it simply means the distance measurement should be in metres and the Guide Number applies to ISO100 film. The Guide Number for a flashgun is useful to know because it will come to your rescue should the meter fail, but since it changes if you measure in metres or feet, or use a film of a different speed, you must keep a careful record.

To bounce light means to point the flashgun at one surface to have it reflected elsewhere in order to light the subject of the photograph. Bounced flash gives nice quality and is often useful for professionals and recommended for amateurs. It gives a soft, shadowless light and is ideal as long as you have enough depth of field for your needs. (i.e. the flash is powerful enough for you to use a stop small enough to get everything necessary in focus). I would never plan my work around the standard idea of bounce because of the necessity of a lowish white ceiling or wall to bounce the light off, and since I do a lot of my work in the dogs' own homes this could never be guaranteed. But if bounced flash works for you it is another trouble-free form of lighting that is suitable for dogs, if rather bland. Some flashguns have a smaller fixed secondary flash that helps to give more life to bounced flash shots.

One way to create portable, semi-bounced, lighting is to use a single flash with a 'bounce head' and an attachment for holding a piece of white card into which you direct the light. This gives a softer light than direct flash, but it is still very directional and gives quite strong shadows, which genuine bounce does not.

The single flash built into the camera is not ideal for dogs, as many people will have found, because it may reflect from the retina of the

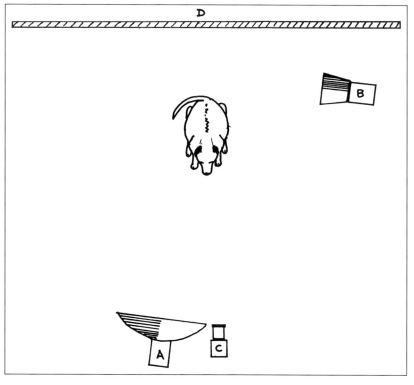

Two light system. *This is the simple two light set-up that I use. The main light (A) is kept as close as possible to the camera (C). The second light (B) is placed high to give back or side light on the dog and also to light the background (D) and kill any shadow from the main light.*

The height of the main light (A) is decided according to the subject but always with regard to the shadow it creates on the background. Where possible the shadow is thrown behind the dog. Lighting is much easier when the background is dark because the shadow does not show.

Three light system. *I use this when I have to light the background such as a room setting. The main lamp (A) is the same as normal but the backlight (B) is adjusted to direct all its light on the dog. The third lamp (C) with a normal reflector is positioned to illuminate the background area. The subject is, of course, well away from the background (E).*

The prime consideration is to get a good pose from the dog – something that frequently seems impossible – and it is essential that a complicated lighting set-up neither distracts the dog nor brings chaos to the session.

eyes, turning them red, blue or green – an effect known as 'red-eye'. This is reduced if the dog does not look directly into the flash, or when the iris of the eye is smaller (for example when the dog is in bright light). Some older dogs with cataracts will always have a bluish tinge to the eye when lit by flash.

A flash on a shoe above the camera will sometimes give red-eye but not always, it depends on the dog's eyes, the exact direction of the flash, and possibly the make of flash gun. Ideally a flash used directly in front of the dog should be positioned at least a foot away from the camera, so that the light is from a different angle, to be sure of eliminating it completely from any dog with normal eyes.

It is impossible, of course, to separate a built-in flash from the camera, but it can be used to fire a slave unit. (A slave unit is a flash which is triggered by the light of another flash) This is feasible, but with a compact camera the aperture is not known so the exposure will be difficult to calculate. Because neither flash (if your second flash is computerised) is designed to be used this way an overexposed picture may result, but this is certainly worth a try for more interesting lighting.

As well as giving red-eye the single flash on the camera will also give a bleak light, rather like a room lit with a bare bulb, and the use of a second light will give a far more pleasant effect. Of course news photographers use one flash on the camera and it is right for their type of picture. A friend has just shown me a series she took with her completely automatic 'flash comes on when it's dark' camera, of her cat tipping over the waste bin and going through the contents; the pictures are fine and unless you are looking for great art there is no reason at all to deride the flat light and shadow that you get from this simple, but easily used arrangement. Some of my advice is perhaps a council of perfection, since many amateur photographers do not need the technical quality, depth of field and sharpness, that are essential for the professional dog photographer.

I seldom use available light (ordinary room lighting), because depth of field is so small with the 6 x 6cm format and a 150mm lens on the Hasselblad. My publishing clients require, first and foremost, a sharp picture. My husband sometimes shoots away between flashes and gets some beautiful results, but they are not often chosen for book illustrations, being rather too arty I think. With ever faster film it is well worth photographing your dog with the natural light in the room. 'Point and shoot' cameras, with automatic built-in flash, give excellent results when mixing flash and daylight in an increasingly sophisticated manner.

If you are taking your dog indoors near a window, and want the garden outside included in the picture, you must expose for the outside as well, by balancing the exposure for both types of light. Failure to do this will leave the garden black with the appearance of night time. It is quite simple – measure the light outside, from inside, (it will be, say 1/ 125th at ƒ8), convert this down, stop and speed, 1/60th at ƒ11, 1/30th at ƒ16, until you get to the correct stop for the flash exposure as metered for your dog. Both outside and dog will now be correctly exposed. The long shutter opening time will not affect the flash exposure, but will expose for the outside scenery. It is surprising how slow a shutter speed you can get away with in these circumstances without camera shake affecting the picture. Automatic cameras may do this mix of flash and daylight for you.

It is informative to watch lighting on television, both indoors and out, and to take ideas from it for photographs. American Westerns show the effect of fill-in light used outside in the strong sun. This is interesting because of the Hollywood, or glamorous, impression that brightly lit shadows give. I have noticed that many picture researchers (who find the pictures for books) choose brightly filled-in pictures, but I have met others who do not like to see any sign of a flash in an outside picture at all. You can also see, on TV, indoor shots with 'every light in the place switched on', and compare it with the beautiful, subtle effects other lighting experts achieve. Studying the lighting on TV can become quite an obsession, but a most educational one.

Electronic flash,in comparison with other types of lighting, is a superb light for photographers of dogs because of its fast speed which enables us to take sharp pictures even if the dog moves. But it is very important to buy a flash with a short flash duration, not longer than 1/ 500th sec and faster if possible. It makes no difference to the power of the flash and you may find that the speed seems incidental to most people; indeed, it may not even be noted in the specification, making it necessary to inquire specifically. Most photographers are happy with the slower speeds, say 1/250th, for everyday work, and if faster flash durations are needed to stop extreme movement in action shots, they use the flash systems that specialise in over 1/1000th of a second. We, as animal photographers, do not normally need over 1/1000th sec, but with speeds under 1/500th we cannot utilise the benefits in photographing the dog when he is not still.

A slow re-cycling time is very irritating because pictures can be lost while waiting for the flash to re-charge. Some makes of flash recycle in under a second while others may take ten seconds or more, so this should be checked before buying.

It is often suggested that I should use flash outside for lighting on a dull day. The main objection to this is that you cannot light the background in a normal scene of fields, hills and sky. If the background is unlit and the dog is lit by flash the background will come out too dark and the picture will look unnatural. You might think that you could give a longer exposure, as in the example above but this is not possible because the dog would move, giving a double image – a moved daylight image   and a sharp flash one. The reason this does not happen indoors is that the dog is lit predominantly by flash, with the daylight only on the garden. It is possible to add a little flash outside to brighten up a dog, but this has to imitate sunlight, and unless your subject is guaranteed to be stationary, enabling you to use a light on a stand, you would need an assistant to hold the flash for you. This to me would be a cumbersome arrangement, but possibly worth trying in some circumstances, though the balance of light would have to be calculated carefully. There is no doubt that some interesting pictures can be taken with flash outside, and it may be worth trying if you like this sort of photography. Many dog show photographers use flash with daylight for all their pictures (particularly in America). It can take away the suggestion of a dull, cold day, and in sunshine can add that touch of glamour, but it has a false look and the photographer must weigh up whether this matters or not. In many cases it does not.

CHAPTER 14

Darkroom work

It is very difficult these days to get good black-and-white printing done, except by professional, and expensive, processing houses. The reason is that the lack of demand from the amateur market has allowed the quality of the black-and-white prints obtainable from the non-professional lab to deteriorate. Amateur photographers interested in black-and-white therefore turn to doing it themselves in their own darkrooms. It is a pity that monochrome is sometimes seen as a poor relation, because it is fun to do and has its place, not just in the realms of art, but also for reproduction in the majority of advertising papers for show dogs. I would hate to be getting no closer to my pictures than viewing them through a strong magnifying glass – the normal way to assess transparencies professionally – and my black-and-white printing, although hard work, reminds me that photographs can still be 'hand made' and have more relevance to a craft show, or perhaps art gallery, than to a laboratory.

Printing your own pictures can be very absorbing. You have time to ponder and regret your mistakes as well as to appreciate a really nice picture as it comes up in the developer. It is you who decides the trim, the size the dog will be in the picture, the degree of tilt to introduce (a very important point), and the whole balance and composition of the picture.

A home darkroom can be set up fairly easily and at reasonable cost – advice is available in books and magazines on the best way to do this so I will not reiterate those instructions here but will concentrate on noting my own methods. Busy and successful dog photographers will have their own systems anyway, so I feel I am speaking to amateurs or would-be professionals who might take on a small amount of work from time to time, not producing hundreds of prints, though possibly doing enough to make a decent and habitable darkroom worthwhile. Although we develop and print black-and-white film ourselves at home, we send all the colour work out. I have very little experience of colour printing because I do not have the time and it is not really an economical proposition, but I can pass on some hints and tips I have learned in my black-and-white darkroom.

Above and Right – *Why print your own pictures? This is the sort of print that you may well receive back from the lab. Nothing overwhelmingly wrong but look at what you can do to make it into a real picture. Always make your print as big as is reasonable if it is for display – a large size gives the appearance of meaning business. Dogs sitting on the table like this really look a bit stupid and unnatural but I took this picture because I knew that, in monochrome, I could disguise it by dark printing. The puppy could not be trusted not to jump down and risk injury, so she had to be held; in my good print I have printed the arm dark and it is easily taken out whereas in the other print this is impossible without a lot of trouble. The quality of tone on the coat is vastly superior in the good print, there is good detail in the whites. Finally the trim is all important – it has assisted in removing the table and the arm as well as making a balanced picture.*

The first and simplest job one can do at home is to develop the film. I have always given slightly longer development times than recommended and find that this gives good results for most dogs, but photographers should work this out according to the enlarger to be used and the type of subject. The temperature of the developer must be right because, in conjunction with the time, it will have a great

Group of Pembroke Corgis showing the making of a picture from difficult beginnings. The lighting is natural sunlight from a conservatory window. The seat was covered with a white sheet because the picture was intended for reproduction and a good contrast was needed between the dogs and the background. The puppies were at an age for mischief and could only be restrained with the owners help. Her hand, the lead, and an area above the seat were subsequently blocked out on the negative, but wherever possible the actual outline of the puppies was left untouched because of the difficulty of painting in the hairy edges. I left the dog's shadow, although it is a little intrusive, because I did not want to draw in the outline of the hair on the big dog's neck.

effect on the negative. Microwave ovens are useful for heating developer, using a plastic or glass measure specially kept for the job, but of course chemicals must never be allowed to come into contact with food.

Obviously you aim for negatives that will print on a Normal grade of paper or Multigrade with a filter of 2 or 2 1/2, so the development time must be adjusted to give the degree of contrast required. Longer development gives greater contrast to the negative. This is useful for dark dogs and dull light – never underestimate the devastating effect of a black dog in bad weather. In extreme circumstances as much as 50% increase in development time would not be too much to get a good negative. Equally a white or partially white dog in strong sunshine can be almost unprintable if too full a development is given as it may be impossible to get detail in the white in the print – but I would only cut development by 25% at the most. This may sound a bit hit-and-miss, but read Ansel Adams' book The Negative if you aspire to perfection! One might think that if a negative is very dense, more exposure could be given in the printing, but a glance at any technical book, with diagrams of characteristic curves, will explain how the whites block up, and instead of detail you get an all-over grey in the highlights. Another reason for trying hard to get good negatives of the right density is to minimise the grain, which increases with a thick negative.

Disasters can be rectified however. An intensifier will increase the density of a very thin negative, and a dense one can be reduced with a mixture of diluted potassium ferricyanide and hypo, or Farmer's Reducer – but always do a test first. Dictionaries of photography will give the chemical formulae if these products are unavailable in shops.

There are many books that describe how to print – a good cheap one is produced by Ilford, available worldwide – so I will confine myself to points on my own work and how they applies directly to dog pictures. I use Multigrade paper; its beauty is that you have so many different grades available in one box of paper. It is used with filters, built into the enlarger or attached below the lens, which give degrees of contrast, from Grade 0 the softest, to Grade 5 the hardest, with half grades in between – 11 filters altogether. Hence the contrast can be adjusted to accommodate the variations of the negative, or creative wishes of the photographer. With dog photography one often has to accept a lack of consistency from one negative to another, due to the changing lighting conditions. Photographers of other subjects may be able to hold up the session until the light is right, but our dogs are liable to pose at their best without regard for such niceties, possibly resulting in a few negatives in the roll requiring harder or softer paper. With the advent of multigrade paper the exact grade required can easily be chosen, and the days of scouring the shops for a few sheets of Grade 4 paper after some nail-biting disaster are gone. Now you can sneak in the 'extra

Below and Right – Ch. Chesara Dark Kruger with Judy Elsden. This picture of the famous Rottweiler has been published many times but always in the version with the plain white background. With the aid of blocking out and contrasty printing a black dog can quite easily be printed in this way, if the background is carefully chosen. The main requisite is that, in the blocking out, you leave the dog's actual outline untouched as far as possible. It is difficult on the small negative to be accurate in the blocking out and I do not like pictures that are obviously painted in. The only area to be made white that actually touched the dog was across the top of the head. Several other dark patches such as Judy's shoes and folds in her trousers also received dye on the negative, after which I used a contrasty paper which left the background white. The tan feet of the Rottweiler tend to be lost due to this contrast but they must be printed darker, and so must the grass around his feet to stop the dog appearing to be suspended in space.

hard' filter and pretend nothing at all is wrong – and the extra hard and extra soft results are very much better than they used to be with fixed grades.

In some circumstances two different filters can be used on the same print or sheet of contact prints. I have used this technique mostly when there are large white highlighted areas; for example, the sun on the coat of a white poodle with the face in the shade. The face was exposed on Grade 2 while the highlit hair was printed-in on Grade 0 to get the texture to show. Skies can also be printed in more easily with a soft grade filter. Glossy paper is used for prints for reproduction, and normally a semi-matt, pearl, stipple, velvet or lustre (according to the manufacturer's label) for the portrait type of pictures that are intended to be framed for the mantelpiece.

As most dog pictures are taken in a hurry it is possible that errors in trim and tilt will have been disregarded at the time. I hate being asked to print the whole negative because I always want to correct my mistakes in tilt, and cut areas that spoil the picture. The tilt must be examined carefully and corrected if necessary. This is frequently overlooked and dogs are allowed to slope, usually downhill, ruining the whole balance of the animal. Tilting the dog up at the front, even more than it really was, is often an improvement. It will give a more upstanding stance and usually does not spoil the position of the feet in conjunction with the bottom of the picture, or make the background look tilted. Naturally any uprights such as fencing or a house must remain upright and the picture cannot be tilted out of true.

With head studies there is even more opportunity for an advantageous tilt, and it should always be tried out when framing-up the print on the

enlarger baseboard. A good general rule for portraits is to make the dog as big as possible and cut out every distraction that you can. Do not be afraid to cut very close at the top, a lot of head room is not necessary, and also crop closer behind the dog than in front, i.e. give a bit of space in the direction in which the dog is looking. A head study should be trimmed to show as good a length of neck as possible.

When my colour transparencies are chosen for publication they go unmasked, just as they are taken, the designer dictates the trim and tilt, and a disappointing job many of them make of it too. I sometimes wonder what they would say if I supplied pictures with the top of the head and feet cut off – but they are quite happy to reproduce them that way in books. My black-and-white pictures are chopped about too but at least I can supply them with a trim and degree of enlargement that pleases me.

I think the secret of good dog printing in black-and-white is to make the prints as contrasty as possible, without losing detail in the white, or letting the shadow detail or dark areas of the dog go solid black. Everything must be done to get the dog to stand out from the background and catch the eye. A study in pale greys will not achieve this unless the picture is specifically designed that way; a dog picture needs to shout at you by means of trim and forceful printing. In this quest for contrast I allow some small areas of white to lack detail at times, (an example is the white feet and chest of a Corgi), in order to get a higher degree of contrast in the rest of the dog, but always ensure, however, that a pale-faced dog does not lose his expression through lack of detail there. Some breeds have beautiful chiselling in the head which is accentuated by shadows under the cheek bones, while others have distinctive wrinkles, frowns and other features which make up their breed type and character. These should all be considered in the printing.

A picture will fail if it loses detail in the black, especially on the face of the dog. Some photographic papers block-up the black and dark greys – the eyes, eye sockets, nose and mouth all go jet black, although the contrast of the rest of the picture may be all right. A softer grade may cure this, or another remedy is to put a thin wash of retouching medium on the black areas, on the negative, to make them lighter, but

Left – *Ch. Miradel Camilla. A subject of this type is quite tricky to photograph and to print. The dog, of course, does not sit in this pose while calculations are made – she plays about, messes up her hair and generally makes life hard for her slaves. So when she does hit the right pose, regardless of the exact lighting or strength of the sun at that moment, technicalities take a back seat. I used Multigrade paper with a normal grade filter, and then printed in the hair on the left hand side that the sun had caught and the top knot, using the softest grade filter (0).*

care must be taken not to get a false effect, a light eye, or an altered expression.

There are great opportunities in black-and-white photography to make changes and correct mistakes. One of the most fruitful is the ability to make certain backgrounds go white. It has always been possible to 'block out' on negatives with a retouching medium, but this necessitates painting round the dog's image and is hard to do well, even with a smooth-coated breed. The other way is to photograph the dog on a background that is basically pale around the dog and to block out all the darker areas, such as a hand or a confusing background. This is especially good where the retouching does not actually have to touch the dog, leaving its outline untouched. All retouching is done on the shiny, non-emulsion side of the negative and can be washed off if not required later.

I like a warm toned paper for dog prints when they are for display, but regrettably I have not succeeded in obtaining a supply of it for my general work since Kodak Bromesko was discontinued. Sepia has become popular again, and more warm tone papers are being advertised. There are ways of mixing your own warmer tone developer, and it may be worth trying if you have time. I now settle for Ilford Multigrade Fibrebased velvet stipple, which I like very much.

Finally a few practical points that I do not often see mentioned. While some things can be very amateurish, others must be to professional standards. It is essential to control film development carefully; the temperature and timing must be exact, the spirals and developing tanks must have no trace of fixer left on them, the container of developer must be shaken before use (then any sediment strained out), otherwise the negatives will not be consistent. Agitation, especially if in smallish developing tanks, must be vigorous and methodical, – patchy negatives will result with the edges thicker (printing lighter) than the centre if agitation is half hearted.

Rules about 'drying in', how the print will look when dry, vary according to the paper. At present I find that glossy multigrade resin-

The prints of these yellow and black Labradors illustrate that in monochrome a background can be reproduced light or dark according to the tone of the dog.

Framing a print or transparency with "L"s to find the best area to enlarge. Two "L"s can easily be cut from card or paper and will assist greatly in 'seeing' the picture.

coated, and, to a lesser extent the fibre-based velvet stipple, must look dark and contrasty in the developer, but slightly less so in the fixer, for it to dry to the correct tone. On the other hand Ilford Galerie and similar portrait types of matt paper must look a little light, but not soft, with no hint of sootiness while in the developer. If you are disappointed with your prints when they are dry, bear this point in mind,

Inexpensive colour prints can be obtained from the high street minilab, photographic shop, chemist or mail order process company. But professional processing houses will supply you with prints that should be better, although they will cost more. Prints are either mass printed by machine or individually hand printed. The hand-made prints are several times more expensive but the main advantage of hand printing is that the picture will be trimmed to your instructions (a 'selective enlargement'), so if you should want only the head, this is the way to do it. An alternative to hand printing, when you require only part of the picture, is to order a machine print (where the whole negative or transparency is always printed) in a larger size than you want. The areas you do not want are then trimmed off. Everyone should have two 'L' shapes cut from card, as shown, to help decide the best trim. Buy a good trimmer; prints can be spoilt by blunt blades, and a good solid trimmer will always cut square and will slice through mounting board neatly, saving time with packing materials. If you post many prints try the new lightweight substitute for cardboard.

Most professional photographers will be quite happy to answer questions about their methods and will be glad to recommend their local supplier to anyone who needs help in finding products not readily available to the amateur.

CHAPTER 15

Which camera?

It is impossible to specify exactly which camera is the best for photographing dogs, but there are a number of different factors to be considered before making a decision about which to buy. First of all the basic differences between the cameras on the market should be understood, then the importance of the features, and how they influence each other can be assessed. For anyone in doubt it is probably better not to go into a camera shop to look around and risk being advised by a well-meaning assistant to buy a camera that turns out to be the wrong one for you. Recently I wanted a cheap camera for my son but I felt so confused by the jargon, initials and claims for the cameras on display in the local shop that I had to leave and sort out the facts at home with a 'which camera' magazine. An example of my difficulty was a camera called 'focus free'. This is not a technical term and might lead a beginner to believe they were getting autofocus – not so, for this was a fixed-focus camera. So often it is what the camera lacks that you need to know about, it is not enough to read of the wonderful features it does have, you must find out what is missing.

The differences between the basic camera types have become less clearly defined with the advances in technology and consumer demand for greater ease of picture taking. The following descriptions cover the fundamentals, although there may be some cameras whose features do not comply exactly with this brief summary. Anyone with experience of photography will be able to make their own decision as to which camera to use but these are some of the points beginners should look for when choosing a suitable camera for photographing their dogs.

I am beginning with the lens because I believe this to be the starting point when choosing a camera for dog photography. One of the first things to realize is that the cheaper cameras are designed with the photography of people in mind. This means that the lens (usually of 35mm-50mm focal length on a 35mm compact or SLR) will give you just the right sized image when taking a person or group, without having to go too close, or very far away. But if you are taking a dog from a normal sort of distance he will come out too small in the picture. You must therefore go in closer to increase the size of the dog. This would be all right if the dog were standing upright, as people do, but he is not; usually he is coming slightly towards you and on four legs. The result of this is that you will get a distorted picture – the head will appear disproportionately large and the hindquarters small, making the dog appear mis-shapen.

It is not the camera, or lens that gives this effect. The eye sees it this way too, but the brain compensates knowing it is interpreting a three-dimensional view and it does not look odd until seen in a two-dimensional photograph. Gross distortion can be seen in racing on television when the horses are filmed in the winners' enclosure, and also on the rare occasion of a dog show being covered, where the dogs invariably look like freaks. In both cases the photographers are usually compelled to use a wide-angle lens because of lack of space.

The answer is to use a lens with a longer focal length, known as long focus or telephoto. Nature photography books often explain that a telephoto lens is for photographing subjects that are a long way off, but they are used also to increase the size of the image when you do not wish to be very close to a smaller than average subject. Unfortunately, this means that the popular compact cameras, because of their fixed, short focal length lenses, are not suitable for dog photography, unless they are of the more expensive type with two lenses or a zoom lens offering a focal length of at least 70mm. The best type of camera for our purposes is one with interchangeable lenses.

To give some approximate figures for lenses suitable for photographing dogs I suggest for the 35mm camera a lens of 90mm or 105mm, or a zoom lens of about 75 - 150mm. For a 6x6cms format camera a fixed focal length lens of 100mm or 150mm; these lenses makes it possible to stand back from the subject and fill the frame without distortion. The actual lens chosen would depend on availability, cost, weight, size and any other photography for which it is needed.

The photographer who has not used a long focus lens before must take more care with technique as there will now be more chance of camera shake, and movement of the subject itself becomes more noticeable. There is also less depth of field, so focusing, and the correct juggling with stop and speed, must be more exact.

When using my Hasselblad with the 150mm lens I have to make a compromise between a fast shutter speed to stop movement, and a small aperture to give sufficient depth of field; with an ISO 100 film, even when the light is not particularly bad, I frequently do not have any speed or depth to spare. On 6x6cm format, 1/250th is the speed I feel happy with, at 1/125th care must be taken, and anything slower is difficult, often leading to camera shake or subject movement. With 35mm cameras a useful formula to remember is that the slowest speed that will stop camera shake is the same as the focal length of the lens in mm, e.g. 1/100 for 100mm lens. For example with a 125mm lens the

This series show the effect of using lenses of different focal lengths – in this case with my Nikon (35mm format) at approximately 1/125 sec. at f8. The two pictures above of the two Labrador Retrievers were taken with a lens of 35mm. The picture on the left shows the distance from the camera to the subject with this lens. The other focal lengths were:
Left and right below – 50mm;
Opposite above – 105mm;
Opposite below – 150mm.

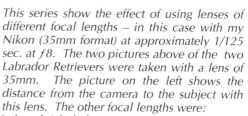

Note the following differences. The background has changed radically. The 35mm lens takes in the whole of the house and the trees to the left. The dogs are distorted, the heads being too large for the body. It can be seen that I took the pictures from the dog's own level and in the picture of them sitting up straight, the distortion is far less noticeable than in the shots where they are leaning only slightly forwards. The 50mm lens pictures are an improvement although I was not very much further from the dogs. The house is getting bigger. 105mm gives good perspective, all distortion is gone and the background is out of focus. We get much the same view of the dogs on the 150mm shot but only a small portion of the house and immediate garden remain. The dark tree that gave one dog a 'hat' with the 35mm lens looms large in the 150mm shot.

slowest speed suitable would be 1/125th sec. Unfortunately it is no good using a tripod as this is too static and anyway it does not stop movement of the subject.

Methods of focusing have undergone a radical change with the introduction of autofocus, but the old methods are still available and favoured by many professionals. The simplest camera, the fixed focus or 'focus free' cheap camera, is really too restricting for dog pictures and only suitable for snapshots. Some people find focusing by rangefinder, as with a Leica M, quick and accurate. Others prefer focusing on the ground glass screen on an SLR with or without the focusing aids provided, and find it easier to judge perspective and framing. Modern autofocus (AF) on SLR and compact cameras is a wonderful aid to the photographer, but, as I have said in the section on taking the photograph, it is less simple than it might appear at first glance. On a 35mm compact it removes the need to worry about focus once the important precepts have been learnt. The more sophisticated and expensive cameras offer different modes of autofocus, designed to stop the photographer using it incorrectly, and to improve the auto-focus performance and usefulness in different, or difficult situations, but they do require to be understood.

The next consideration is how the exposure will be measured, and set, on the camera. For the serious dog photographer control over the exposure is very important as I discussed in Chapter 12. With many traditional cameras exposure is set manually by the photographer, judged with anything from a simple calculator to a separate meter, such as a Weston. The results are as good as the calculations and the experience of the photographer. At the opposite extreme is the automatically computed exposure, without controls (except sometimes a plus or minus setting), as found on the majority of 35mm compact cameras. This is easy to use and can produce successful pictures, but the photographer is unable to choose the speed and aperture settings.

More versatile are the automatic programmed exposure modes, as seen on many modern SLR cameras. The camera selects the speed and aperture according to the predetermined program which is set; it could be 'Action', 'Portraiture' or many of the other styles of picture one might take – but I have yet to see 'Dogs'!

The type of shutter in the camera is important to experienced photographers because there are advantages and disadvantages in the two types, focal plane or between-lens such as the Compur. The focal plane, which is normal for 35mm single lens reflex, and some non-reflex cameras, limits flash synchronization with electronic flash to shutter speeds of 1/125th or sometimes up to 1/250th. These shutters however have very fast speeds available when flash is not used. Between-lens, including Compur shutters as used in the Hasselblad, allow flash synchronization at any speed, but their top speed is not as high as that of focal plane shutters. The advent of electronic shutters has rather blurred the distinction and in many instances the exact type of shutter is not specified in modern compacts. However it is worth knowing the limitations in shutter design so as to avoid mistakes when choosing a camera.

Obviously the more you understand the camera's technicalities the better are the chances of getting the right equipment together. Do not make the kind of mistake I did when I bought the new (at the time) Hasselblad 2000FC body for its faster shutter speeds, only to find that, although it was compatible in many ways with the lenses from previous models, it was not completely so in one aspect, which affected my way of working. My prism viewfinder exposure meter gives readings in EVs which I then set on the lens, but when the C lens is used on bulb (as it must be to open the Compur shutter, to allow the new system's focal plane shutter to function) the EV scale is inoperative. I stuck a note giving equivalent stops and speeds for EV ratings on the lens hood, but towards the end of a busy day my brain would seize up. Luckily a colleague is happy with it for fashion photography and I have gone back to the earlier model, doing without the faster speeds. The more sophisticated the camera becomes, with automatic exposure and autofocus, the more the variations and programs have to be thought through, assessed and understood. Tests of the systems should be obtained from magazines and the problems liable to be encountered have to be identified.

Like many professionals' cameras, my Hasselblad has few gadgets and no programs, so I have to concentrate to achieve good results. The main thing to remember is that expensive lenses produce clearer, sharper pictures, and the Rolls Royce cameras are beautiful to use; but there is no magic, everything works according to basic laws. You cannot buy more depth of field nor a camera that will enable you to use a fast shutter speed all the time.

For those wanting great ease of use, above all else, the autofocus compact is a good choice, provided it is a two-lens model with one lens of at least 70mm focal length, or a similar zoom lens. Some zoom compacts go to longer focal lengths than 70mm. In a compact I would suggest looking for a high maximum shutter speed (which the camera sets for itself in bright light), a plus or minus exposure adjustment, fill-in flash (these cameras all have built-in flash, though not all with a fill-in facility), as well as provision for switching the flash on and off, an auto focus system of the best quality (as many steps as possible). Decide if you need a lens with a large maximum aperture, which is useful if you intend to take a lot of pictures in bad light without flash, e.g at indoor shows. Then consider shape, weight and different loading systems, backlight compensation and the possibility of extras like a hot-shoe for using additional flash lamps. But it will be seen that these

35mm auto focus compacts do not have provision for setting the shutter speed and aperture because the exposure is all automatic, not fixed but computed, and this will not allow the control many people might wish for. The essence of the compact – simplicity, the loss – versatility.

For photographers wishing more control there is the large group of manual focus, non- reflex cameras with a variety of specifications, many of them now available on the secondhand market. But it is the ubiquitous single lens reflex that so many people have aspired to – it is the professionals' camera and that says it all. I cannot begin to describe the features of these last two types of camera as they would fill a book on their own; information is readily available from magazines or the various manufacturers.

When I chose the Hasselblad, at the beginning of my career, it was the only camera that fulfilled all my needs. I wanted 2 1/4" (6 x 6cm) square format, interchangeable lenses and a Compur shutter to synchronise with flash at all speeds. When a lens, with its between-lens shutter, is removed, the film in the camera must be protected from the light, so a second shutter becomes necessary. This is the feature that made the Hasselblad such an important camera. There are now

Below – The black Labrador, Oscar, as well as demonstrating the lenses, gives us a lesson in posing. His ears and expression are so much better in the right-hand picture. Both these photographs are taken from human eye level. In the picture on the left I stood very close looking down on the dog using a 50mm lens. It shows distortion which gives the dog a large head, thin legs and a barrel body. With an 80mm (right), still from a high viewpoint but taken from further away, one gets a far more attractive angle. One can see here that a wider angle lens gives the feel of the dog coming out of the picture towards you; some styles of photography make use of this but, in general, I dislike a distorted picture of a dog.

several similar versions of the Hasselblad concept, some have automatic metering and the price makes them very attractive. The grass is always greener on the other side of the fence and when my original Hasselblad was stolen I decided to give up such a traditional camera and I tried out some of these newer ones. I was rather intrigued with their automation and was tempted by the chance to have two lenses for the price of one. Suffice to say that I subsequently bought a 500C Hasselblad, secondhand but in mint condition, as similar as possible to the one I had lost. I now use this camera with a prism viewfinder and built-in exposure meter, a 150mm, a 250mm and a seldom-used 80mm lens. Having strayed from the fold I now have great respect for the Hasselblad, and appreciate the design, engineering and particularly the balance, which I found lacking in the others. There are, of course, updated versions of my model which bring many advantages but it is 'horses for courses' in dog photography and my 500C Hasselblad suits me extremely well.

Many great photographs are taken on 35mm and publishers are accepting this format without question, but I still prefer to use 2 1/4" square for most of my photography. Some years ago I decided that I might as well make use of the advantages of 35mm and my Nikon is a useful camera for action and similar work. I chose the FE, after careful consideration because it had the features I needed, although it is not from the professional range. It has aperture priority – you set the aperture and then check the speed in the clear viewfinder display, juggling both, by turning the aperture ring, to get the best combination for the subject. I would rather do this than have a programmed camera decide it for me. Probably the best feature of 35mm is the range of zoom lenses available which are so well suited to dog photography, and if I ever change my style of photography to a more journalistic or reportage approach, then the lightness, ease of use and versatility of 35mm would probably win me over – but the sacrifice of the Hasselblad's pure quality would be hard to accept.

For my real holiday snaps, though not for dogs, I have a little Russian 35mm camera. The Zenith Lomo has a good lens, automatic computed exposure, manual focusing, and in addition provision for flash photography with manual aperture settings coupled to a shutter speed of 1/60th sec – all at a completely give-away price! My experience has been that if you read up on cameras carefully, with regard for your own needs and a knowledge of the features, you soon find that one will emerge as the best for you.

Technological advances come more and more quickly and we shall have to learn the extent to which they will assist us in making even better pictures of our dogs. But it is not cheap to keep up with the latest advances and we should remember that we still have our brains to make the calculations, eyes to focus and fingers to set the camera.

Tailpiece

It's odd that so few books have been written about photographing dogs – they are, after all, man's best friend and surely deserve better than this. There are hundreds of books on nature photography but there must be more people wanting to take a good picture of their family dog than of fungii in the woods.

Many photographers today are taking beautiful pictures in difficult circumstances, so I don't know why the general standard of dog photography is so variable, even among some professionals. Many of the pictures I see in dog books and magazines are of far worse quality than those found in books on birds or wild animals, so why is such poor photography of dogs accepted?

It is my greatest wish that the subject should be taken a little more seriously, not only by photographers but also by publishers and picture researchers who sometimes seem uninterested in finding pictures that show the character and beauty of our friend the dog. In some ways amateur pictures, always taken and shown with such affection, demonstrate more feeling for a dog, although unfortunately they often fail in technical quality.

I hope that this book will help my fellow dog owners and enthusiasts to get some good pictures. It has not been my intention to be very technical but in some instances it has been necessary. Equally though, because it has been written for so many of my friends who say that they haven't the least idea how a camera works and never will, it may seem in places too basic and obvious to more experienced photographers.

My photography was learned in a world of commercial and fashion work, and when I began my training many years ago we had tungsten lighting, whole-plate cameras, and an army of retouchers to remove every wrinkle from the clothes. Now we have computerised electronic flash, 35 mm colour film is normal, the retouchers' work is minimal and wind machines ruffle the garments. The world of photography has changed in many ways since then but , above all, there is a welcome free and easy attitude to picture taking.

In spite of my strictures on portraying show dogs and the tedious problems of exposure I hope that the fun of photographing dogs is reflected in this book. My view is that once photography is understood then the rules can be broken and pictures can become more exciting.

Writing this book has been all enjoyment and pleasure. I think photographers are always looking for a sitting-down job – a change from all day on their feet – it has forced me to think through some of my ideas, rather like learning to be a dog judge, and it has also reminded me of the recent innovations in photography and how much there is to help us on the technical side.

Most books of this sort mention the changes that will undoubtedly come to assist us further to take good pictures. I love gadgets and new inventions, but I remember my friend Charles Brown, the great aerial photographer, with his old camera (I read that it was a Zeiss Palmos bought for £17 before the first World War) and I wonder if he really would have liked an autofocus zoom – he might well have – but his pictures could hardly have been improved upon.

Publisher's note

*Two more titles by Sally Anne Thompson
are in preparation for this new series:*

Photographing Horses
Photographing Cats